Revitalizing the Commons

OTHER BOOKS BY C. A. BOWERS

Cultural Literacy for Freedom (1974)

The Promise of Theory: Education and the Politics of Cultural Change (1982)

Elements of a Post-Liberal Theory of Education (1987)

The Cultural Dimensions of Educational Computing: Understanding the Non-Neutrality of Technology (1988)

Responsive Teaching: An Ecological Approach to Classroom Patterns of Language, Culture, and Thought (1990) (with David Flinders)

Education, Cultural Myths, and the Ecological Crisis:Toward Deep Changes (1993)

Critical Essays on Education, Modernity, and the Recovery of the Ecological Imperative (1993)

Educating for an Ecologically Sustainable Culture: Rethinking Moral Education, Creativity, Intelligence, and Other Modern Orthodoxies (1995)

The Culture of Denial: Why the Environmental Movement Needs a Strategy for Reforming Universities and Public Schools (1997)

Let Them Eat Data: How Computers Affect Education, Cultural Diversity, and the Prospects of Ecological Sustainability (2000)

Educating for Eco-Justice and Community (2001)

Detras de la Apariencia: Hacia la descolonizacion de al educacion (2002)

Mindful Conservatism: Rethinking the Ideological and Educational Basis of an Ecologically Sustainable Future (2003)

Rethinking Freire: Globalization and the Environmental Crisis (2005) (co-edited with Frederique Apffel-Marglin)

The False Promises of Constructivist Theories of Learning: A Global and Ecological Critique (in press)

Revitalizing the Commons

Cultural and Educational Sites of Resistance and Affirmation

C. A. Bowers

LEXINGTON BOOKS

A division of
ROWMAN & LITTLEFIELD PUBLISHERS, INC.
Lanham • Boulder • New York • Toronto • Oxford

LEXINGTON BOOKS

A division of Rowman & Littlefield Publishers, Inc.
A wholly owned subsidiary of The Rowman & Littlefield Publishing Group, Inc.
4501 Forbes Boulevard, Suite 200,
Lanham, Maryland 20706

PO Box 317
Oxford
OX2 9RU, UK

British Library Cataloguing in Publication Information Available
Library of Congress Cataloging-in-Publication Data

Bowers, C. A.
    Revitalizing the commons : cultural and educational sites of resistance and affirma-
tion / C. A. Bowers.
        p. cm.
    Includes bibliographical references.
    ISBN-13: 978-0-7391-1334-9 (cloth : alk. paper)
    ISBN-10: 0-7391-1334-8 (cloth : alk. paper)
    ISBN-13: 978-0-7391-1335-6 (pbk. : alk. paper)
    ISBN-10: 0-7391-1335-6 (pbk. : alk. paper)
    1. Commons. 2. Natural resources, Communal. 3. Community power.
4. Globalization. 5. Education and globalization. I. Title.
    HD1286.B69 2005
    33.7—dc22   2005027605

Printed in the United States of America

♾ ™ The paper used in this publication meets the minimum requirements of American
National Standard for Information Sciences—Permanence of Paper for Printed Library
Materials. ANSI/NISO Z39.48-1992.

Contents

Preface vii

1 Introduction 1

2 The Road Not Taken: Education's Complicity
in the Enclosure of the Commons 17

3 Revitalizing the Commons of the African-American
Communities in Detroit (with Rebecca Martusewicz) 47

4 Community-Centered Approaches to Revitalizing
the Commons 85

5 Understanding the Commons within the Context
of Contemporary Ideologies 107

6 The Choice Before Us: Educational Reforms That
Revitalize or Further Enclose the Commons 139

References 169

Index 173

About the Author 187

Preface

The threats to what remains of the world's diverse cultural and environmental commons represent a unique challenge to Western universities, particularly since what these universities have designated as high-status knowledge has played such a dominant role in undermining both the cultural and natural commons. The challenges today are to understand the range of threats to the commons, to recognize the possibilities within our own rural and urban areas for revitalizing the commons, and to recognize and support the efforts of non-Western cultures.

The following chapters are intended as an introduction to the complexity of the world's commons, and the role that education can play in helping to resist their further destruction. Thus, the first chapter will be used to address the nature of the commons as they existed in the past, as well as what remains of the commons today. Understanding the current threats to the commons needs to take account of the many ways in which today's industrial culture contributes to the enclosure of the commons, the threats to the commons in both the northern and southern hemisphere by international institutions such as the World Trade Organization, and by the Western scientific, technological, and educational approach to development. Lastly, the ways in which contemporary ideologies support and undermine the commons need to be more carefully examined, especially since Western universities reinforce the use of a political language that is based on the same deep cultural assumptions that underlie the current efforts to globalize the Western industrial model of production and dependency upon consumerism.

The drive to turn every aspect of daily life into a market opportunity has not entirely succeeded. In the face of intensive indoctrination and economic pressure to abandon the commons for a monetized lifestyle, which ends in even deeper levels of poverty for many people, important aspects of the commons within our own culture as well as that of non-Western cultures still remain resilient. A sign of hope is that the defenders of these commons are no longer being silenced by a Western-imposed sense of inferiority. Even in Western cultures where great ingenuity and economic resources have been used to expand markets and to introduce new technologies, the commons still exist. Many aspects of these commons, however, are in constant danger of being replaced by new forms of commercialism and exploitation.

The chapters that address the prospects of revitalizing the commons should not be read as a romantic appeal to return to a past that the world has moved beyond. Rather, they will be used to explain how the traditions of thinking that were constituted in the West before there was a general awareness of environmental limits continue to limit our ability to recognize both the importance of the commons and the many ways in which they are currently being undermined. The ways in which language, particularly the language that is reinforced in public schools and higher education in the West, continues to reinforce an industrial mode of consciousness will be a primary focus. Another focus will be on how computer-mediated thinking and communication affect the intergenerational knowledge that is essential to sustaining the commons. Another set of concerns that will be given attention is the double bind connected with the nature of the knowledge that universities in the West have designated as high-status—and the way in which the face-to-face, non-monetized intergenerational knowledge has been marginalized or completely silenced. The knowledge promoted by universities involves a double bind in that it has made important contributions to the well-being of humankind, while at the same time it has created a growing state of dependency upon many technologies and conveniences that are degrading both the environment and the ability of people to be less dependent upon monetized activities and relationships.

Lastly, attention will be given to identifying the activities, social groups, and policies that still exist at the local level that represent the ongoing intergenerational renewal of the commons. Why these commons sustaining traditions have a smaller adverse impact on natural systems will also be examined. While it has become fashionable in some quarters to write off the public schools and universities as incapable of being reformed, I will make the case that this is entirely too pessimistic—while also admitting that resistance will be hard to overcome. Given the rate of environmental change being caused by economic globalization, what choice do we really have but to make the effort? The reforms I will suggest will address how the university traditions of inquiry and historical knowledge can be adapted to the task of understanding the forces that are undermining the commons—through cultural colonization, technological hubris, ideologically and linguistically based silences, long-standing Western myths of progress, natural economic laws, and a human-centered world. I will also suggest the role that public schools and universities can play in mapping the changes occurring in natural systems as well as the intergenerational skills and knowledge of how to develop personal talents and interests that strengthen involvement in community.

In many ways the books I have written before have led to making the revitalization of the commons a central focus of educational reform. As there is always the danger of repeating oneself, especially when one writes on the assumption that the readers will likely not have read any previous books, I have not gone into some topics as fully here as some readers may desire. Thus, if there is an interest in a more in-depth discussion of the how language reproduces earlier cultural ways of knowing, and how this brings into question the widely held myth that individuals are autonomous thinkers, I suggest that *The False Promises of Constructivist Theories of Learning: A Global and Ecological Critique* (2005) be read—especially the chapter that challenges the idea that students construct their own knowledge. For a more in-depth discussion of how universities determine what constitutes high- and low-status knowledge, *The Culture Denial: Why the Environmental Movement Needs a Strategy for Reforming Universities and Public Schools* (1997) should be looked at. The extended discussion of why environmentalists and people working to revitalize the commons should be regarded as the genuine conservatives, and the so-labeled conservatives that want to reduce everything to a market relationship and to promote a survival of the fittest form of individualism should be regarded as liberals, can be found in *Mindful Conservatism: Rethinking the Ideological and Educational Basis of an Ecologically Sustainable Future* (2003). And the discussion of the connection between educational reforms that address eco-justice issues and the revitalization of the commons is developed in *Educating for Eco-Justice and Community* (2001). A more extended examination of how computer-mediated thought and communication reinforce an industrial/consumer-oriented form of consciousness can be found in *Let Them Eat Data: How Computers Affect Education, Cultural Diversity, and the Prospects of Ecological Sustainability* (2000).

As in the past, I am indebted to a number of people who have shared their insights and recommendations of authors who are addressing similar issues. At the same time I am totally responsible for the interpretations, extrapolations, and silences in this book. Another major source of support has been my wife, Mary Katharine Bowers. Through the years she has been steadfast in helping to keep the environmental crisis a central focus in my discussions of educational reform. I am also indebted to the Foundation for Deep Ecology for a grant that has helped to support the publication of this book.

Chapter One

Introduction

The prospects of humanity, as I shall argue here, lie more in the revitalization of a cultural practice that was understood by the earliest humans who occupied the savannas of Africa than in the ideas of the techno-utopian thinkers who are now predicting that the emerging computer phase of the evolutionary process will eliminate all the ills, injustices, and strife that now seem so central to human experience. The revitalization of this ancient cultural practice, which became known in the pre-Roman occupation period of Britain as "the commons," is also a more life sustaining cultural practice than what is envisioned by the current proponents of economic development, educational reformers, and neo-liberal politicians who have been mislabeled as conservatives.

What was this ancient cultural practice that is still part of daily life in every culture in the world—even in the most technologically developed? And how does the revitalization of the commons enable us to think about social justice issues in ways that address the cultural roots of the ecological crisis? The answer to these questions requires withholding the formulaic judgments that too often are made, especially by academics, whenever the suggestion is made that we can learn from the cultural practices that had their origins in the ancient past. Considering how the revitalization of the commons represents a far more radical proposal than what the followers of Marx, Freire, and the new class of techno-utopian thinkers have to offer requires setting aside another expression of formulaic thinking promoted by a Western university education. That is, that each new development in modern culture requires leaving traditions behind—except for holidays and religious observances.

Indeed, a deeper understanding of the commons will reveal that even the most technologically "advanced" communities (the Palo Altos of the

Western and non-Western world) still depend upon the commons as the basis of their physical and social existence. This dependence exists in spite of another cultural practice that can also be traced back at least a thousand years. In anticipating the contemporary mentality that promotes the continued destruction of the commons while making self-assured pronouncements about the dangers of romanticizing indigenous cultures and traditions, I want to say at the outset that this book is about the contemporary threats to what remains of the commons in various regions of the world. The focus of the book is also on current efforts to revitalize the commons by activists in Western and non-Western cultures. What they are attempting to resist is the techno-industrial culture that, like a rapidly mutating virus, continually seeks to transform what remains of the commons into new market opportunities. In considering the examples of communities that are resisting this transformation, with its accompanying spread of poverty, we shall also see examples of affirmation that are much-needed sources of hope.

The commons have traditionally been understood as the environment that is available for use by the entire community. This included the rivers, forests, pasture, wild animals, plants, and so forth. In short, the commons included all of the environment that sustained human life. The commons, even in ancient times, also included the air that people breathed, the language they spoke, the narratives that intergenerationally renewed their sense of identity and values, the craft knowledge and technologies that had been refined over generations of living within the limits and possibilities of their bioregion, the norms and structures that were the basis of their decision-making processes, their games as well as their forms of aesthetic expression, their knowledge of the medicinal properties of plants, and so forth. In effect the commons encompassed every aspect of the human/biotic community that had not been monetized or privatized. Another key feature of the ancient commons was that it required local systems of decision making (which did not always meet the West's standard of social justice— which in practice falls far short of its own rhetoric).

The purpose of identifying both the natural and cultural commons that were (and still are) shared by the community is not to romanticize their various practices; nor is it to make sweeping generalizations about how various social systems represented traditions of exploitation and abuse. Rather, it is to provide the conceptual basis for recognizing the aspects of the commons that are still viable in a modern, technological, and consumer-dependent culture. A second purpose is to highlight the ecological and eco-justice importance of resisting the further destruction of the commons in both Western and Third World cultures. A third purpose is to clarify how the commons continues to be transformed by another tradition that can be traced back to the Statute of Merton which was enacted in AD 1235. This statute provided the earliest legal basis for the process of enclosure in Britain. But the process of enclosure in other cultures goes back much farther in time. Enclosure also took many different forms, depending upon the culture's political system and thus its distribution of power.

The enclosure of the commons, a concept and practice that needs to be understood as having particular relevance to our own times, involved transforming what was communally shared into what is privately owned and monetized. That is, enclosure involves the monetizing of what previously could be used by the members of the community on a non-monetary basis. This transformation alters the communal practices where work is reciprocated and where much of daily life is based on a barter or mutual exchange system. The process of enclosure meant that communal access is restricted in ways the benefited, generally on a monetized basis, the owner of the land, water, and so forth. Enclosure, and what has come to be called "the tragedy of the commons" where a member of the community attempted to expand his herd, fish catch, or other practice, at a rate that, if everybody were to follow the practice, would overwhelm the sustaining capacity of the natural systems, has been avoided by indigenous cultures such as the Quechue of the Peruvian Andes, the Papago of the American Southwest, and the indigenous cultures of Mesoamerica.

In the modern, industrialized West, enclosure has taken on new forms of expression that have radically reduced the cultural and environmental commons. This, along with the dominant belief system that privileges the interests of the individual over all other relationships, has become a major reason for the rapid degradation of the environment—and to the undermining of the traditions of self-sufficiency of other cultures. In addition to the transformation from what is communal to what has become private property and thus requires participation in a money economy, various forms of enclosure have also transformed the process of decision making—and thus the local system of accountability. The decisions about the use of the commons are generally made locally, whereas the process of enclosure, which often involved ownership by someone or a corporation that does not have to live with the consequences of its decisions, undermines local democracy.

The destruction of the commons, in both Western and non-Western cultures, needs to be understood in terms of what has now become the dominant characteristics of the Western approach to development. Indeed, the word "development" is synonymous with the modern processes of enclosure. It is achieved through the relentless drive to transform what remains of the commons into exploitable resources and thus into new markets. And it is justified on the grounds this expansion of consumerism is governed by the law of supply and demand that dictates the direction that progress will take. It is also assumed that these market forces have the same standing in the natural order of things such as the earth's gravity and other natural phenomena. While the Western approach to equating the enclosure of the commons with progress has benefited certain classes of people, it has also resulted in many more people becoming increasingly dependent upon an economic system that they have little control over, and that too often replaces a subsistence level of existence with impoverishment and debilitating diseases that are a result of being unable to earn a living wage.

Bonifil Batalla, an anthropologist and political activist who has worked on behalf of the right to self-determination of the indigenous cultures of Mesoamerica, raises the question that is becoming increasingly important to Third World cultures that are now being pressured to adopt the Western model of development. In response to the question of "what does a self-sufficient (subsistence) economy have to offer?" he states that

> it offers basic security, a broader margin of subsistence in difficult years, even though one has only what is really indispensable. Various crops, together with wild plant gathering, hunting, fishing, and the raising of domestic animals, intermixed with some sort of handicraft production (pottery, basketry, and many other products), and the generalized capacity for other sorts of work such as construction and maintenance—all offer a broad spectrum of possibilities that can be altered or combined, according to the circumstances. No one of these possibilities alone, given the conditions of indigenous communities today, assures survival. Together, however, they offer an acceptable margin of security. For this multiple strategy to succeed, each activity must be on a small scale, producing what is necessary and nothing else. (1996: 28)

Both the question and Batalla's response also have increasing relevance for individuals and communities in the most industrially developed regions of the world.

The spread of the modern forms of enclosure, and their "survival of the fittest" consequences, make the importance of basic security from dire impoverishment especially important to a larger segment of industrialized societies. The modern expressions of enclosure (privatization and monetization) can be seen in the way many aspects of daily life that previously were met in intergenerationally connected families and communities have now become part of the industrial culture. The industrialization of health care, education, production and preparation of food, play, entertainment, and even thought and communication now cost more than many individuals and families can afford. The extent of this problem can be seen in the level of borrowing in the United States, which is now just over 20 trillion dollars a year, that is required to sustain the industrial/consumer-dependent lifestyle.

Enclosure even extends to altering the daily cycle of light and darkness, with some scientists now investigating how the increased exposure during the night to the light of urban areas may be diminishing the effectiveness of the body's immune system. Another often overlooked aspect of the natural commons—namely, the silence that is the background of natural sounds, is similarly being impacted (enclosed) by the spread of industrial culture. And in scientific laboratories around the world, the race is on to alter the genetic make-up of plants and animals in ways that bring more of our food supply under the control of market forces. Even the airwaves have become enclosed, as corporate ownership now allows them to be used largely by inane television programs to hold the attention of the viewing public long enough to present a blitz of commercial advertising—which is equally mind numbing. The privatization of the commons is now being extended to include what was previously the public's right to water provided by municipal and thus non-profit systems as well as such other basic services as waste treatment. The replacement of municipal- by corporate-owned water systems is taking place across North America, and in countries such as Britain, New Zealand, South Africa, Argentina, Chile, Mexico, India, Malaysia, Nigeria, and Ghana. Indeed, there are fewer and fewer biological processes and cultural activities that remain untouched by the spread of industrial culture.

These modern forms of enclosure magnify the same basic dynamics that were present in the earliest acts of enclosure in rural Britain. That is, enclosure benefits the few at the expense of the many, while local decision making is replaced by owners and elites who are seldom members of the community and thus do not have to be accountable to their neighbors or live with the consequences of their decisions. And as the basis of the local economy (which may operate on reciprocal exchange and barter systems) is further undermined there is a growing sense of insecurity as well as the antisocial behavior that accompanies impoverishment and a sense of hopelessness.

These are sweeping generalizations. To many readers who take the conveniences and now necessities of an industrialized existence for granted, these observations may be interpreted as not only being misinformed but also lacking in an appreciation of the many benefits derived from modern science and technology. In anticipating this response, I must say that I am not discounting the many contributions that modern science and technology have made to improve the quality of everyday life. This acknowledgment needs to be made in order for readers to recognize that my basic argument is for revitalizing the commons in order to bring about a better balance between the self-sufficiency of individuals, families, and communities and the market forces of supply and demand that are now assumed to operate as natural laws that govern all human relationships. Self-sufficiency, as Batalla points out, provides a measure of basic security at the local level, and it is the basis of local democratic decision making. Both are now being threatened by the spread of market forces that are sanctioned by international laws and treaties, and by powerful centers of financial and political power such as the International Monetary Fund, the World Bank, and the World Trade Organization.

The critics of the idea of revitalizing the commons are likely to frame the basic issues we face in an entirely different way. That is, since we can now travel to nearly any place in the world and have access to industrially prepared and mediated food, medicine, education, entertainment, and information, the critic is likely to pose a different series of questions: Why should this process of industrializing the commons be withheld from any culture? Don't we have a responsibility to share the benefits of a scientific, industrial lifestyle with the less developed peoples of the world? And don't we have a responsibility to overturn, even through the use of military force if necessary, the traditions of other cultures that resist being incorporated into a world economy and consumer-dependent lifestyle? These questions are likely to be viewed as the more relevant ones, particularly by people that take for granted the Western myth that progress is linear and driven by scientific discoveries and technological innovations. They are most likely the people who have not become part of the statistics of the unemployed, or had their retirement funds disappear as a result of corporate fraud and mismanagement. Ironically, the myth of unending material progress goes largely unchallenged even by people whose expectations of a secure economic future are now being adjusted in the face of the new economic realities that the myth cannot explain.

Just as the pharmaceutical industry can only increase its profits by creating in the public the fear of pain, illnesses, bodily malfunctions (which its products supposedly will alleviate or cure), the Western myth of unending material progress and economic growth is dependent upon a public that accepts without question that they need the latest technological innovation or change in product design—from the latest shoe by Nike to the latest upgrade in digital technology. Fostering the sense of need, which is the primary mission of the multi-billion-dollar advertising industry, leads to the further exploitation of the environment and to higher levels of toxic wastes that now foul the neighborhoods of the marginalized cultural groups—as well as the self-renewing capacity of natural systems. By representing needs in terms of the acquisition of material goods, rather than in terms of meaningful social relationships and the development of personal talents that make a contribution to the quality of life within the community, the industrialization of what remains of the commons creates another problem that E. F. Schumacher warned about in *Small Is Beautiful*—a book that needs to be read by each generation. As he put it,

> The cultivation and expansion of needs is the antithesis of wisdom. It is also the antithesis of freedom and peace. Every increase of needs tends to increase one's dependence on outside forces over which one cannot have control, and therefore increases existential fear. Only by a reduction of needs can one promote a genuine reduction in those tensions which are the ultimate causes of strife and war. (1973: 31)

The way of achieving the basic security for the members of indigenous cultures that Batalla writes about also supports Schumacher's observation that needs (that is, artificially induced needs) must be limited if dependence upon outside forces is to be reduced. Suggesting that many subsistence cultures possess a wisdom that may be unattainable in the West, given its deeply held assumptions about the ability of experts to manage every crisis and to continue to meet the needs of a consumer-dependent public, does not mean that the answer for Western cultures is "to go back" in an effort to copy the wisdom of indigenous cultures. Going back is not an option. The indigenous cultures of the world took different paths in their approach to development, and thus should not be viewed as

having attained only a "primitive" stage in a linear and evolutionary pathway that we now occupy as the more advanced culture. The profound
differences in the mythopoetic narratives that separate indigenous cultures from the formative mythopoetic narratives in the West make it
impossible to use them as a model for our future development. However,
we can learn from them in ways that will help us to recognize the importance of the commons, and how to revitalize it. And the need to learn
from them about what constitutes the basic human priorities becomes
clearer as we understand just how insecure an increasing number of
people in the West are becoming. Many millions of people around the
world have been reduced to meeting their basic needs through what can
be salvaged from the local waste disposal sites. Even the members of
the middle class that previously took for granted their place on the escala-
tor of industrial progress are now beginning to realize that their economic
future is no longer secure. While the middle class in the United States,
Canada, and other Western countries has not been reduced to such dire
economic circumstances as now being faced by the world's extremely
impoverished, the rate of long-term unemployment has been increasing—
along with bankruptcies and even homelessness. Children in America now
experience more of their parents going through bankruptcies than through
divorce.

As the lives of people in the West become even less centered on the self-
sufficient possibilities of the commons, and more in the industrial culture
that is beyond their control, their insecurity becomes more palpable. The
introduction of the microchip and the information technologies it has
spawned, along with international trade agreements, has moved the industrial process to a new level of influence over the lives of people around the
world. In addition, the nature and scale of enclosure has changed in fundamental ways. During the earliest phase of the Industrial Revolution and
the liberal tradition that gave it conceptual direction and moral legitimacy,
enclosure took the form of corporate ownership of natural resources and
the monetization of labor (at the lowest possible level). The need then was
for vast numbers of workers who lived in the slums surrounding the factories. The inefficient infrastructure that connected the colonies of that era to
the factories, and enabled goods to be shipped to distant markets, continued to fuel the need for workers. While automation in recent years, especially across America's farmland, led to reductions in the need for
workers, there was a recent (and temporary) expansion in the need for

workers to build the infrastructure for the new information technologies essential to the emerging global economy.

This achievement, however, has created greater insecurity in the lives of workers—both here and abroad. The new information technologies not only provide near instantaneous communication between corporate headquarters and production sites located in different regions of the world, as well as enable them to gather information on changes in markets and the flow of vast amounts of money, they also make possible the movement of production facilities to more profitable foreign sites—without regard for the impact on local communities. And when a factory is located in a low-wage region of the world, and the workers are housed close to the factory and thus separated from their families and communities, there is a disruption in the intergenerational systems of knowledge and skills that are the basis of a subsistence existence. The workers thus become dependent upon a money economy that may disappear when the factory is moved to an even more economically promising location. The commons also suffer from the toxic wastes that result from the production process.

The continuing transformation of what remains of the commons in different regions of the world is based on a number of other trends that are creating further insecurity—and even poverty. These trends include the unrelenting drive to carry the process of automated production to the point where few if any workers are needed, the "outsourcing" of production to the regions of the world where a modicum of social stability and a guarantee of low wages exist, the new laws that are now internationally enforced that allow corporations to patent and thus claim ownership of gene lines of plants and animals, and the neo-liberal ideology that is now encoded in international laws that allow organizations such as the World Trade Organization to shield corporate investment from democratic decision making at the local and national level. How these trends now poise a further threat to the commons can be seen in the following examples—which can be multiplied many times over.

A central feature of the ideology that underlies industrial culture is that greater efficiencies are essential to greater profits, which leads to expanding the search for new technologies and markets. In short, the expansion of industrial culture is the primary measure of social progress. The "invisible hand" that supposedly ensures, like the process of natural selection, that the most efficient technologies will prevail over the less efficient has been fundamental to the Western approach to production. This logic has also led to the near total marginalization of the workers' ability to make decisions about how the production process should be carried out. With this function now under the control of management, the current drive is to turn the power of critical reflection to the task of developing more automated technologies that will further reduce the need for workers—and by extension the need to pay health care and retirement benefits. If we examine the changes that automation has brought to different sectors of the economy (agriculture, industrial production, service) in recent years it is difficult to refute the fact that the trend is toward a radically smaller work force, one that has less security, lower wages, and fewer health and retirement benefits.

The industrialization of agriculture is a prime example of this trend. Over a seventy-year period the American farm population has been reduced from just over seven million family-run farms to just under two million—even as the U.S. population has more than doubled. Currently, the industrialization of agriculture has led to a mere 50,000 farming operations producing 75 percent of the food consumed by Americans (Kimball 2002: 55). The side effects of this drive to achieve greater efficiencies include the loss of rural communities, the contamination of groundwater with fertilizers and pesticides that are the mainstay of industrial agriculture, the exploitation of migrant foreign workers, and the expenditure of vast amounts of public resources for the purpose of subsidizing agribusiness. The destructive impact of industrial agriculture also includes the spread of rural poverty as the cost of production increases in response to the need to acquire the ever more expensive farm technologies. In short, both the human and natural communities (the commons) are casualties of this shortsighted form of progress.

The industrialized approach to fishing is having an even more catastrophic impact on the world's oceans—which should be regarded as one of the more important life-sustaining commons that humans have historically relied upon. A recent report in *Nature* summarizes the changes in fish populations that have occurred over the last forty years. Following an intensive study of 13 of the world's major fisheries, it was found that the number of large fish (tuna, swordfish, cod, and flatfish) had been reduced by 90 percent. Even the increase of other species that filled the ecological niches left by the disappearance of the large fish were found to decline after an initial expansion in their numbers (Myers and Worm 2003: 280). As fish are a major source of protein for much of the world's population, the rate and scale of changes occurring in the ocean ecosystems are especially alarming.

Scientists are now beginning to understand that the cultural practice of catching the larger fish is leading to a shift in the process of evolution itself, with the gene pool being altered by the growing predominance of smaller fish that are unable to reproduce the robust characteristics of the larger fish. This shift, in turn, undermines the ability of the depleted fisheries to return to the previous levels—as is now being experienced with the codfish populations off Newfoundland's Grand Banks.

The cult of efficiency that drives the automation of the workplace has led to the loss of employment in other sectors of American society. Jeremy Rifkin's book, *The End of Work* (1995), has been largely overlooked as it appeared just as the building of the information technology infrastructure was in full swing, and the need for workers seemed on the verge of exceeding the number available. But as we can now see, this was a temporary phenomenon that created a false understanding of the future of the American worker. With the new computer-based technologies spreading into every sector of the economy, the trend toward fewer and less secure work opportunities has accelerated. Lifetime employment, what the middle class took for granted for decades, is now a thing of the past. Even the new class of highly paid "knowledge workers," as Rifkin refers to the people who run the information technologies, are finding that they are being made redundant by the technologies they helped to create. Accompanying the displacing of workers through automation is the decline in the real earnings of workers. Today, in many instances both members of the household must work in order to achieve the same standard of living that previously was attained by a single wage earner.

The future of the automated workplace can be seen in recent developments. The list of corporations that have increased production through automation, while reducing their immediate- and long-term expenses for human workers, include Goodyear, General Electric, General Motors, and Boeing—to cite just a few. The connection between the efficiencies gained through automation and a radical reduction in the number of workers can be seen in how AT&T was able to handle 50 percent more calls with 40,000 fewer workers. The ideal of the fully automated and thus worker-free workplace has been achieved by the Victor Company in Japan. There 65 robots perform 150 different assembly and inspection tasks that previously required 150 workers. Now only two workers are needed to oversee that continuous functioning of the robots. Automation has even affected employment in smaller work settings such as the logging operations in Great

Britain and the United States. A machine called the "feller buncher," which can be operated by a single worker, now does the work that previously required 10 to 15 workers.

The future of employment in the digital phase of the industrial revolution we are now entering is further threatened by a new phenomenon associated with the role that information technologies play in creating the global economy. The threat goes by the seemingly innocuous name of "outsourcing." Manufacturing facilities are increasingly being moved overseas to whichever country has the lowest wages and the least restrictive environmental regulations. Corporations that originally moved their production facilities to Mexico and now moving them to China and other countries in Southeast Asia. The fate of Mexican workers and their communities does not figure into these corporate decisions. The same attitude now prevails in the decisions by major software companies that are outsourcing their research projects to India and their chip production facilities to other countries in Asia. The economic logic that drives outsourcing can be seen in the comparison between the salary of an American software programmer (approximately $80,000 per year) and the salary of an overseas programmer, which is approximately $20,000 per year. Given the similar differences in other sectors of the economy between the average wage of workers in America and in countries such as India and China, it is now estimated that in the next 10 years no fewer than 3.5 million jobs in the financial services and high-technology industries will be outsourced.

The outsourcing of industrialized work to other regions of the world is destructive of the commons in ways that are not generally recognized when only the impact on wages and employment is considered. In addition to raising the level of unemployment and underemployment (which has a greater impact on non-whites) there is also the ongoing marginalization of the intergenerational knowledge that previously was the basis of a less consumer-dependent lifestyle. The importance of this knowledge, as well as its complexity, has largely been ignored as our educational institutions have prepared students to expect that all the necessities and non-necessities of life—food, health care, entertainment, leisure activities, and so forth—can be supplied by the industrial process, and that employment would give them access to this supposed cornucopia of unending plenitude.

The myth promoted by the educational institutions promised that if individuals directed their energies toward advancing up the salary scale and promotional ladder they would experience an increasing amount of happiness and convenience beyond what they could imagine today. The myth also provided a formula for living their non-working hours as consumers of home entertainment systems, drivers of SUVs, and participants in outdoor activities—all of which required constant attention to purchasing the latest upgrades in the technologies that seemed to validate the myth as the everyday reality that normal people could expect to continue. With the constant message of industrial culture being that technological progress is synonymous with human existence itself, there was no need or interest in learning from the intergenerational fund of knowledge that in earlier times provided for the development of personal talents and skills that were the basis of non-heavily monetized family- and community-centered lives. And in not knowing how to prepare a meal that uses non-processed ingredients, to use the medicinal properties of plants, to play a musical instrument, to repair an electrical or plumbing problem, to mentor others in activities that have a smaller ecological footprint, and so forth, reliance on the industrial culture of ready-made products and experts became a necessity—even as it made individual lives less secure and fulfilling.

The outsourcing of the industrial mode of production to Third World countries, while it allows workers to perform their repetitive tasks in cleaner environments, is having the same intergenerationally disruptive impact. In many instances, the workers are housed together in barrack-like settings, and are thus cut off from their families and local communities. And in being separated physically and conceptually from the network of activities, knowledge systems, and reciprocal relationships within their communities they enter the double bind of the industrial mode of existence. That is, they become dependent upon a monetized lifestyle that offers them no guarantees of future economic security, while at the same time they become isolated from the intergenerational knowledge of the environment and patterns of mutual support that provide a modicum of security from poverty and want.

The spread of industrial culture is now undermining the commons in even more destructive ways. While the privatizing of water has a long history, particularly in the American West, the neo-liberal ideology that guides the policies of the International Monetary Fund and the World Trade Organization has led to water being turned into a marketable commodity on a worldwide basis. Cultures that previously regarded water as sacred, as well as those where poverty is so deep and widespread that the need to purchase water now creates a special hardship, have not been immune from the spread of corporate ownership of what previously was the right to the water as a member of the commons. Municipal water systems, which are examples of the commons within urbanized cultures, are now being taken over and run by corporations. Giant corporations such as Vivendi Environment and Suez Lyonnais des Eaux (with sales of 17.1 and 5.1 billion dollars respectively) now transport water to countries where it is in especially short supply. The growing demand for drinkable water, which reflects the degraded condition of local water systems, is leading corporations to exploit local aquifers at a rate that threatens the local citizens' immediate and long-term need for water. The market for bottled water, for example, is now doubling every two years, and with the massive profits this brings to corporations there is little interest in considering water as part of the heritage that needs to be passed on to future generations.

The biological diversity and intergenerational knowledge that have been part of the commons for hundreds of thousands of years are also being brought under the industrial system of private ownership, mass production and marketing, and the increased drive for higher profits. The worldwide legal infrastructure recently put in place now allows for the patenting of industrially modified organisms, as well as the patenting of indigenous knowledge of the medicinal knowledge of plants. The effect has been to undermine local knowledge systems, and to force people to purchase what previously was part of the commons and thus freely available to all the members of the community. The patenting of the different chemical properties of the neem tree in India is the most famous example of what Vandana Shiva refers to as the West's biopiracy of Third World indigenous knowledge (1996). For hundreds of years the villagers used the neem tree for a variety of purposes— as a toothpaste, in the preparation of soap, for curing leprosy and diabetes, as a contraceptive, for fuel and the production of methane, and as an insecticide. The patenting (privatizing and thus enclosure) of the various chemical properties of the neem tree meant that what was previously freely available to the villagers now had to be purchased in the form of a commodity. In effect, the worldwide enforcement of intellectual property rights, such as a patent owned by an international corporation, brings more of the commons under the control of industrial culture. The impact on local communities is to force them to participate in a money economy, which they too often lack the means to do. Any discussion of the industrial system and the money economy that it requires needs to recognize that an estimated 2 billion of the world's population lives on two dollars or less a day.

For these people, as well as the growing number of technologically displaced workers in the West, reliance on the networks of mutual support, as well as access to the life-sustaining biodiversity of the commons, is essential to providing a measure of security against poverty. But there is more than security that is at stake. By defining wealth in terms of money and thus in terms of access to material goods that must continually be replaced by the latest innovation, what is considered as wealth is actually a source of impoverishment as the need to work long hours and sometimes at two jobs leaves little time or energy for participating in symbolic aspects of the commons. Participating in community festivals and theater, playing an instrument and writing poetry, working in community gardening projects, helping others in making house repairs, participating with others in a group quilting project, and so forth, leads to a wealth of relationships and meaning. It is a form of wealth that avoids the problem of needs that Schumacher warns us about. That is, the wealth of being a participant in the life of the community reduces the dependence upon the outside forces over which the individual has little control. Furthermore, it is a form of wealth that reduces the need to be as fully dependent upon consumerism as is the case where being caught in the cycle of working to stay ahead of the mounting burden of debt leaves many people with little energy to do anything other than sit in front of the television—and become further victimized by the commercials that now dominate television programs.

Our educational institutions now play a central role in expanding the influence of industrial culture in the lives of people in the West and in Third World countries. Whether they can be reformed in ways that contribute to revitalizing the commons, and thus to nurturing both the Earth's ecosystems and cultural diversity, is one of the major challenges we face today. And whether they can be reformed in time is another question that we will not have the answer to until it is too late. In the next chapter I will examine how our educational institutions, those engines of progress, contribute to undermining the diverse commons of the world. I will also attempt to clarify why current proposals for reforming our educational institutions, in being based on ethnocentric and pre-ecological ways of thinking, are unlikely to even address the destruction of the commons. In the following chapters I will present examples of the grassroots, community-centered efforts to revitalize the commons that can serve as a basis for understanding the nature of the educational reforms that must be undertaken. These sites of resistance and affirmation represent models of life in the post-industrial cultures that can be sustained by the Earth's ecosystems. They are also models that provide a more useful guide to educational reform than the neo-liberal assumptions about the efficacy of the autonomous individual, the progressive nature of change, and the anthropocentric worldview that educators, politicians, and corporate leaders continue to rely upon.

Chapter Two

The Road Not Taken: Education's Complicity in the Enclosure of the Commons

The deeply held prejudices that set the educated elites in the West apart from the subsistence cultures that continue to live more by the traditions of the commons, as well as keep them from actively participating in the urban commons, can be traced back to the Greek philosophers who established a competing tradition, one that represented abstract rational thought as the means of attaining knowledge that is uncorrupted by daily experience and cultural context. From Plato to the present, Western philosophers have relied upon this tradition of abstract thinking to argue about the nature and source of knowledge, the role of language, and the basis of values. Richard Rorty's arguments about the virtues of the self-creating "ironist" individual, as well as his criticisms of traditions, are only the latest example of ignoring the diversity of cultural knowledge systems and the actual patterns of daily experience. The road taken by Western philosophers privileged print over the spoken word, the individual's potential to be a rational and supposedly an autonomous thinker over the intergenerational, place-based knowledge of the community, the Western way of knowing over non-Western ways of knowing, and the purposive rationality of experts over the supposedly chaotic and mindless forces of nature. This varied and contested tradition of rationality has led to important achievements, particularly in laying the basis of a democratic, checks and balances system of governing, and in the development of the sciences and useful technologies. Unfortunately, many of these achievements are now being brought into question by changes occurring in natural systems that, until recently, went largely ignored because of the prejudices in the thinking of Western philosophers and in the different interpretations of the Judeo-Christian tradition of thinking.

Public education in the West, unlike the origins of Western universities, was and still is justified on the grounds that it is essential to the expansion of industrial culture. In fact, the earliest classrooms were modeled on the English factory system. And today, the connections between public schooling and the industrial, consumer-dependent culture are being made even closer through the use of computers in the classroom. Universities, on the other hand, had their origins in the religion-dominated late Middle Ages, and thus have only recently (in the last hundred years or so) become aligned with the values and ways of thinking that are dominant in industrial culture. Even though a university education was for many years understood as contributing to the life of the mind, and thus regarded the pursuit of wealth and the engagement in an industrial-based lifestyle as reflecting a fallen state of existence, it is now regarded as essential to economic success and to personal advancement within the higher echelons of industrial culture.

This radical transition in how the value of a university education is now understood has not, however, affected the cultural prejudices that can be traced back to the earliest Greek traditions of abstract rational thought. Some readers may criticize this generalization as ignoring the traditions of empiricism and, more recently, phenomenology. However, this criticism would be misdirected, as these supposedly nonrational approaches to knowledge were dependent upon rational arguments. The empiricism of John Locke, and its later formulation as part of the scientific mode of inquiry by John Dewey, continue to ignore other cultural ways of knowing, the influence of language in reproducing earlier, culturally specific patterns of thinking, and the ways in which the traditions of a culture are reenacted as part of daily experience. David Abram's *In the Spell of the Sensuous* (1996) is an exception to the rational discussion of the nature of phenomenology, and Alasdair MacIntyre's *Whose Justice? Which Rationality?* (1988) represents one of the rare exceptions to the tradition of ethnocentrism that has been the hallmark of Western philosophers.

The many prejudices carried forward and given legitimacy by Western philosophers are now being questioned—but not by philosophers who are still under the influence of the old ethnocentric orthodoxies that continue to dominate most departments of philosophy. These prejudices can still be seen, though in muted form, in the writings of the small group of philosophers who are beginning to address environmental issues. For example, a massive anthology edited by Andrew Light and Holmes Rolston III, which contains 40 essays by the leading environmentally oriented philosophers and published under the title of *Environmental Ethics* (2003) does not contain any essays that consider other cultural approaches to environmental ethics. Nor are there any references to the nature of the commons, the varied nature of the intergenerational knowledge that represents sources of resistance to industrial culture, and the ways in which the language of a culture carries forward the moral values that we too often misrepresent as based in the rational thought process of the individual. Gregory Bateson, the Western thinker who best understood that intelligence is influenced by the interpretative frameworks (cultural maps) carried forward in the culture's languaging processes and involves an interactive relationship with the environment (which many indigenous cultures have understood for centuries), is not even mentioned. In short, even the environmentally oriented philosophers cannot escape reproducing the historical prejudices that have made Western philosophy largely irrelevant to sustaining the commons and to understanding the cultural forces that are transforming it into market relationships.

For readers who think I am wildly off the mark in making these observations, I invite them to elicit the responses of students (even graduate students) who are majoring in philosophy—even environmental philosophy—to the questions raised before: What is the nature of the commons, and in what ways does it have relevance to the quality of everyday life? Are the commons only characteristic of Third World cultures, or do they also exist in densely populated urban areas such as London and Los Angeles? Who are the mentors in their community? What needs to be conserved in this era of ecological uncertainty? In what ways do Western universities contribute to undermining the commons of the world's cultures?

Even if students understand what is meant by the commons, it is unlikely that they will have encountered any extended discussion of its history, its transformation through enclosure, and its current relevance to the issues they discuss in their environmental philosophy classes. It is also likely that their own personal experience rather than any discussion in their classes will be the basis of their answer to the question about the mentors in their community. Indeed, it is the rational thought of the individual, which is an expression of hubris learned in philosophy classes, that makes it unnecessary to learn from mentors. The prejudice that leads to ignoring the importance of mentors is based on the idea that the traditional knowledge, skills, and values that are the basis of mentoring are constraints on the expansive and progressive power of rational thought.

The question of what needs to be conserved in an era of ecological uncertainty is likely to be understood by only a few students. And they will have definite ideas about the ecological uncertainty part of the question. The part of the question relating to conserving traditions that are more ecologically sustainable will more likely be interpreted as too reactionary to be given serious consideration. Given the tradition within Western philosophy of claiming that the ability to use rational thought in ways that produce wisdom, and that establish the basis of human values and ways of knowing, it is surprising that the question about what needs to be conserved has not been a central concern. The rationally constituted theories of reality, as produced by Plato, Aristotle, and Descartes, as well as the empiricist theories of Locke and Dewey have been used to justify reactionary political regimes, and to further the process of Western colonization. But the political uses of their ideas should not be confused with conserving ecologically sustainable cultural practices and values. Both Plato and Aristotle have been used to justify authoritarian regimes, and the ideas of both Descartes and Dewey have been used to justify the spread of Western science as the only legitimate approach to knowledge. While some might argue that these are conserving patterns, particularly in terms of power relationships and the suppression of dissent, they should be more properly understood as totalizing regimes of thought. Asking what needs to be conserved that is ecologically sustainable involves considering how the place-based intergenerational knowledge and practices within both rural and urban settings contribute to lifestyles that have a smaller ecological impact. The question cannot be answered with a universal prescription that would be consistent with Dewey's experimental inquiry or the ideas of other Western philosophers. Rather, the answer would have to come from within the culture itself. In other words, the answer would have to take account of the knowledge of the local ecosystems—or what remains of them.

The prejudices that are so basic to the thinking of Western philosophers are examples of traditions, and carrying on these traditions by subsequent generations of philosophers is an example of a conserving process. But few philosophers understand that the word "tradition" encompasses every aspect of culture that is passed on over four generations or cohorts. Nor do they recognize that their professional careers, as well as most aspects of their personal lives, involve the reenactment (and even modifying) cultural traditions. In spite of how the reenactment of cultural traditions is an inescapable aspect of their daily life, they nevertheless continue to think of tradition as the source of backwardness, the absence of rational self-direction, and what needs to be overturned by the exercise of rational thought. This prejudice, which has its origins in the use of language that has for hundreds of years been disconnected from the context of how people live their lives, continues to be reproduced in philosophy classes. One of the consequences is that students will not be engaged in a culturally contextualized discussion of the nature of tradition. The result is that they will not be aware that the democratic process should involve the interplay between critical thinking and a deep and complex understanding of the traditions that are the basis of civil society, the community patterns of mutual support and self-reliance, and the conservation of the commons.

The last question that I am suggesting as leading to evidence that philosophy students, in following their professor's approach to wisdom, are totally unprepared educationally to address one of the root causes of the ecological crisis is the one about how Western universities contribute to undermining the commons of the world's cultures. This question goes to the heart of the process of economic and technological globalization—and to the Western universities' complicity in the current drive to transform the world's cultures in ways that model the Western individually centered, consumer and technologically dependent lifestyle. How many graduates of Western universities understand how the forms of knowledge, as well as the process of encoding this knowledge, are based on Western assumptions about the autonomous nature of the individual, the progressive nature of change, the culturally neutral nature of language and technology, and the progressive and myth destroying nature of Western science? If university graduates were asked to identify and explain the importance of the forms of knowledge that universities have relegated to low status through the practice of excluding them from the curriculum, I would expect to encounter few informed responses. That most forms of knowledge excluded from the university curriculum are especially important to living less consumer-dependent lives is likely to be of little concern or interest to students.

The two points that need to be emphasized here is that by socializing students to the taken-for-granted importance of high-status knowledge the universities are promoting the spread of industrial culture. The connections between high-status knowledge and the globalization of the West's industrial culture can be seen in the characteristics they share: an emphasis on the form of individualism that views the traditions of community as a source of backwardness, the importance of literacy and other abstract systems of representation that marginalize the importance of context and cultural differences, a conduit view of language that reinforces the idea of objective knowledge and thus the nonmetaphorical nature of the language/thought connection, the emphasis on technological solutions that are represented as culturally neutral, the assumption that change is inherently progressive and linear in nature—thus representing traditions as a barrier to progress, the reliance on the scientific method as the most reliable approach to knowledge and values—a view being promoted by E. O. Wilson and others who now argue that natural selection governs how cultures develop. Secondly, the deep cultural assumptions underlying high-status knowledge make irrelevant the need to learn about other cultural knowledge systems—especially the knowledge systems that have kept market-oriented activities in balance with other aspects of daily life.

These four questions could be asked of students in the other academic disciplines and professional specializations—economics, sociology, political science, psychology, history, computer science, business, education, and so forth. Given the heavy reliance of environmental studies on the sciences, I strongly suspect that the number of graduates who could make informed responses to these questions would increase only slightly. My questions are not only intended to highlight the silences and distortions in a Western university education; they are also intended as research and dissertation topics.

Before critics dismiss my arguments about how public schools and universities in the West contribute to the further enclosure of the commons they need to consider the proposals being made by leading scientists and computer futurist thinkers who are graduates of our leading universities. Their contributions to the futurist literature are especially important, as many of them are highly acclaimed in their field of science and computer technology. Their well-established reputations in the fields of science and technology give greater legitimacy to their futuristic predication, with few of their readers being aware that their writings on the future are sheer speculation dressed up as scientifically based evidence. E. O. Wilson is a leading example of a highly regarded scientist who has attained near guru status as a spokesperson for environmental causes. Francis Crick, Richard Dawkins, Stephen Hawking, Ray Kurzweil, and the late Carl Sagan are other examples of scientists who are promoting what can only be called scientism of the most problematic sort. Their extrapolations, predictions, and pronouncements on which cultures need to be replaced by a culture that fits their own ethnocentric ways of thinking would, if carried out, further undermine the diversity of the world's commons. In addition, their supposedly scientifically based predictions of future cultural change serve another important political function—namely as an ideology that justifies the globalization of industrial culture. Unfortunately, few members of the public, including university graduates, are aware of when the predictions of these scientists move beyond the realm of science and onto the slippery slope of scientism and ideology. Just as the scientifically based industrial mode of production promotes homogeneity, the nonscientifically based predictions of these scientists contribute to the conceptual homogeneity that Vandana Shiva warns against in *Monocultures of the Mind* (1993).

THE ONE TRUE SOURCE OF KNOWLEDGE

The denigration of the knowledge systems of other cultures can be seen in the following observations by such prominent scientists as E. O. Wilson, Carl Sagan, and Stephen Hawking. In *Consilience: The Unity of Knowledge* (1998), Wilson dismisses the possibility that non-Western cultures have achieved any form of significant knowledge. As he put it, "today, the greatest divide within humanity is not between races, or religions, or even as widely believed, between the literate and illiterate. It is the chasm that separates the scientific from prescientific cultures. Without the instruments and knowledge of the natural sciences . . . humans are trapped in a cognitive prison" (p. 45). Later in the book, Wilson announces that evolution now makes it possible for the cultures of the world to escape from another cognitive prison—their religious beliefs that conflict with the most recent findings of Western science. Wilson acknowledges that the creation of religion is an adaptive behavior that contributes to the genetic success of a group, but he goes on to claim that the scientific understanding of evolution now makes it possible to replace these poorly adapted belief systems with a new sacred narrative. As Wilson's judgments about the knowledge systems of other cultures, as well as his own uncritical acceptance of the messianic role of scientists, are driven more by hubris than genuine knowledge, it is important to read his own statements.

The idea of a genetic evolutionary origin of moral and religious beliefs will be tested by the continuance of biological studies of complex human behavior. . . . *We cannot live without them.* . . . People need a sacred narrative. . . . If the sacred narrative cannot be in the form of a religious cosmology, it will be taken from the material history of the universe and the human species. That trend is in no way debasing. The true evolutionary epic, retold as poetry, is as intrinsically ennobling as any religious epic. . . . That is the only way to provide compelling moral leadership. Blind faith, no matter how passionately expressed, will no longer suffice. Science for its part will test relentlessly every assumption about the human condition and in time uncover the bedrock of moral and religious sentiments. (pp. 264–265, italics in the original)

A similar condition of extreme hubris that led scientists down the path of measuring human intelligence, promoting eugenics, and now, using the new biotechnologies to create chimeras (including the implanting of human DNA in the eggs of other animals) seems not to have altered Wilson's faith in the ability of scientists to assist Nature in the process of cultural triage and to provide the moral leadership that is in line with the process of natural selection.

Carl Sagan's reputation rests more on his celebrity as a media promoter of scientific achievements and the possibility of space travel than as a major scientific discoverer. And in this role, his writings take on special significance. For the public that is largely unable to recognize when he moves beyond a lucid explanation of new scientific discoveries to turning science into an ideology, his writings contribute to the myth that Western science represents the one and only valid approach to knowledge. In *The Demon-Haunted World: Science as a Candle in the Dark* (1997), Sagan acknowledges that while scientists in the past have made mistakes, they nevertheless possess the only valid approach to knowledge. In order to not misrepresent his argument for making Western science the basis of all the world's cultures, it is important to read his own words.

One of the reasons for its success is that science has built-in, error-correcting machinery at its very heart. Some may consider this an overbroad characterization, but to me every time we exercise self-criticism, every time we test our ideas against the outside world, we are doing science. When we are self-indulgent and uncritical, when we confuse hopes and facts, we slide into pseudoscience and superstition. . . . We insist on independent and—to the extent possible—quantitative verification of proposed tenets of belief. We are constantly prodding, challenging, seeking contradictions or small, persistent residual errors, proposing alternative explanations, encouraging heresy.

We give our highest rewards to whose who convincingly disprove established beliefs. (pp. 30 and 34)

There are a number of assumptions that stand out in this summary of the advantages of Western science over other knowledge systems: science is self-correcting; when critical thought is missing, confused and incorrect thinking takes over, and the mission of scientists is to "disprove established beliefs." This is an incredible list of self-promotion virtues. Sagan sees no need to qualify his statements in ways that correctly identify the legitimate domains of scientific inquiry, and the aspects of culture where it is clearly wrong to assess ideas and values in terms of "quantifiable verification." By ignoring the limits of scientific knowledge, Sagan, like Wilson, contributes to the perception that if the world's cultures are to move beyond their current "demon-haunted" state of existence they must adopt Western science as their only guide to knowledge and values.

Stephen Hawking, who holds the same prestigious Cambridge University chair that Isaac Newton held in 1663 and is invited to speak at scientific meetings around the world that are addressing the most advanced thinking in theoretical physics, carries the reductionism of science to an even greater extreme. In his widely read book, *A Brief History of Time* (1998), he states that when physics finally settles on a theory that unifies the standard model of particle physics with general relativity (that is, comes up with a "Theory of Everything") it will be possible to use the resulting mathematical model to explain everything. With the Theory of Everything, he writes, "we shall all, philosophers, scientists, and just ordinary people, be able to take part in the discussion of why it is that we and the universe exist" (p. 175). More recently, Hawking told an interviewer for *Focus* magazine that in light of the threat posed by the rapid advances in artificial intelligence, and the danger of it surpassing human intelligence, scientists should develop the technology for increasing the complexity of the human DNA and thus the level of human intelligence.

In effect, Hawking has moved the discussion of knowledge systems beyond the Promethean role that Wilson and Sagan assign to scientists who are supposedly able to transcend the deepest, taken-for-granted assumptions of their own culture. The members of the various cultures of the world will soon be challenged by the Theory of Everything to set aside their own cosmologies, and to derive from the collection of mathematical symbols a more accurate understanding of why they exist, their purpose in the larger web of life, and the values they should live by. Hawking's promise that scientists will soon provide the basis for cultures to obtain their true bearings is so cosmic in scope that it is difficult to see how it could be introduced into the present or future political discourses. But on a more worldly level, where people's health and future prospects are being undermined by the failure of politics and the rapid degradation in ecosystems, Hawking's extrapolations on the answers that will shortly be found in the discoveries of Western scientists further strengthen the modern prejudice about the irrational foundations of other cultural knowledge systems. To recall Sagan's way of explaining the basis of their plight—they live in a "demon-haunted world" and only Western science can bring the light into their everyday lives.

EVOLUTION AS AN IDEOLOGY THAT PROMOTES A WORLD MONOCULTURE

The world now seems to be afflicted by a series of conceptual distempers that are driving the political process in different parts of the globe. American Christian fundamentalists are fixated on events in the Middle East, looking for signs of the final fulfilling of Biblical prophecy and the end of history. The followers of Sayyid Qutb, perhaps the most influential Islamic thinker of the twentieth century, are rejecting Western liberalism in favor of returning to what is now being represented as the original purity of Islam, when the code of shariah governed all aspects of community life. And the debunkers of non-scientific knowledge, such as E. O. Wilson, Carl Sagan, Richard Dawkins, and Francis Crick are promoting evolution as the explanatory framework for understanding globalization as the outcome of natural selection. The central concern of these three groups is not on improving the lives of the billions of people who are attempting to live on two dollars or less a day, nor is it on the need to revitalize the commons as an alternative to the increasingly environmentally destructive nature of industrial culture. It might be thought that if the followers of Qutb are successful in getting a significant number of the world's population to return to the seventh-century lifestyle of Islamic culture, the impact of industrial culture would be significantly reduced. Similarly, if the Christian fundamentalists are right about God's plan for the coming rapture, it might be thought that the exploitation of the environment for the purpose of amassing material wealth will be radically mitigated. However, both the Islamic and Christian fundamentalist visions are based on going back in time to recover an earlier promise of a God-directed life. For the Christian fundamentalists, the word of God has been filtered through a number of translations of the Bible by men from different cultures, and thus different ways of knowing. For both groups of fundamentalists, the attempts to make the present fit the past represent reactionary movements.

The debunkers of non-scientific knowledge, on the other hand, are promoting a form of conceptual distemper that the future can only be understood in terms of the theory of natural selection. The chief proponents of what can be called evolutionary fundamentalism are E. O. Wilson and Richard Dawkins, and, in the techno-utopian camp, Ray Kurzweil. Wilson gives the clearest explanation of how the process of natural selection determines which aggregate of brains (culture) survives, and which will go extinct. While he tries to finesse the argument so that is does not appear as a case of genetic determinism by claiming that human development is governed by "gene-culture convolution," he continually repeats the primary casual connection in the following way:

> The genes prescribing the epigenetic rules of brains and behavior (culture) are only segments of giant molecules. They feel nothing, care for nothing, intend nothing. Their role is simply to trigger the sequence of chemical reactions within the highly structured fertilized cell that orchestrate epigenesis. Their writ extends to the level of molecule, cell, and organ. This early stage of epigenesis, consisting of a series of physiochemical reactions, culminates in the self-assembly of the sensory system and brain. Only then, when the organism is completed, does mental activity appear as an emergent process. *The brain is the product of the very highest levels of biological order, which are constrained by the epigenetic rules implicit in the organism and physiology.* (1998a, p. 165, italics added)

Wilson then goes on to restate the basic tenet of evolutionary fundamentalism that governs all organisms: "Brains that choose wisely possess superior Darwinian fitness, meaning that statistically they survive longer and leave more offspring than brains that choose badly" (p. 165). In an earlier passage in *Consilience*, Wilson states without qualification the determining role of the environment. As he puts it, "through natural selection, the environment ultimately selects which genes will do the prescribing" (p. 137).

The diversity in cultural ways of knowing—including how people experience meaning, the values they base their lives upon, and their sense of self-identity—do not lend themselves to empirical observation and thus to quantifiable evidence. Even though this subjective dimension of experience is largely inaccessible to science, Wilson and the other promoters of evolution in other disciplines (Ellen Dissanayake in art theory, J. Allan Hobson in psychology, Martin Weitzman in economics, Irene Wilson in theology, Arthur Wolf in anthropology, Daniel Dennett in philosophy of science, Ray Kurzweil in computer science, and Brian Swimme in eco-cosmology) are relentless in their efforts to make it a total explanatory framework. They all avoid referring to the "survival of the fittest," the phrase made popular by earlier Social Darwinists. Nevertheless, their collective efforts are just as easily translated into the ideology that current neo-liberals can use to justify social policies that give special advantages to large corporations. Thus, natural selection becomes the reason for the elimination of small producers as well as the cultures that resist the forces of globalization. It can also be used to explain why the commons are disappearing under the pressures of industrial culture. The argument that the environment selects which genes—and by extension which brains and thus which cultures—will survive means that the politics of self-interest are now the driving force. Yet there is a basic problem with how the theory of natural selection can account for the survival of a hyper-consumer based culture that is undermining the viability of the Earth's ecosystems. That is, why are the cultures that have lived within the limits of their bioregions now being selected for extinction? Wilson and the others do not explain why the design process of Nature values a world monoculture rather than selects in ways that foster cultural diversity—which is the operative principle in the biological realm.

The argument that the environment selects the genes that, as Wilson put it, "prescribe" the capabilities of the brain and thus the thoughts and behaviors we associate with culture is more a matter of faith than supported by scientific evidence. Wilson's evolutionary fundamentalism is further buttressed by the claim that the brain is a machine, which is a view held by Francis Crick and other scientists studying the "mechanisms" of the brain. According to Wilson, "the surest way to grasp complexity in the brain, as in any other biological system, is to think of it as an engineering problem" (1998a, p. 102). The profound political and moral implications of this statement are also ignored by computer scientists such as Hans Moravec and Ray Kurzweil who share Wilson's evolutionary fundamentalism, as well as his way of thinking of organic and cultural phenomena as mechanism that can be re-engineered. To borrow Hawking's phrase, evolution is their "Theory of Everything." Their only difference with Wilson is in their claim that the brain is a primitive computer, and that it is being replaced in the evolutionary process by computers that will not possess the limitations of biological organisms, such as illness and death. According to Kurzweil, who reiterates Moravec's argument that we are entering the "postbiologi- cal" phase of evolution, computers will program themselves to have human-like personalities, to have religious experiences, and by continu- ally updating their programs they will make the human phenomenon of death as extinct as the dinosaurs (1999, pp. 128–129).

According to these evolutionary fundamentalists, brains are machines, values and religious beliefs are "hardwired" (to use Wilson's phrase [1998b]), and culture is a collection of "memes" that must meet the same test of Darwinian fitness—that is, survive longer and leave more offspring. In terms of cultures, this means leaving more "memes" that will replicate themselves over the generations to come. According to Richard Dawkins, who describes individuals as "survival machines" that exist for the sole purpose of ensuring that the genes can replicate themselves over as many generations as possible, memes are to culture what genes are to biological organisms. And like genes, memes must meet the same test of natural selection. That is, the environment determines which memes are better adapted and thus will survive—and which will disappear. Dawkins explains the similarity in the following way:

> memes are tunes, ideas, catch-phrases, clothes fashions, ways of making pots or building arches. Just as genes propagate themselves in the gene pool by leaping from body to body via sperms or eggs, so memes propagate themselves in the meme pool by leaping from brain to brain via a process which, in the broad sense, can be called imitation. If a scientist hears, or reads about, a good idea, he passes it on to his colleagues and students. He mentions it in his articles and lectures. If the idea catches on, it can be said to propagate itself, spreading from brain to brain. As my colleague N. K. Humphrey neatly summed up in an earlier draft of this chapter "memes should be regarded as living structures, not just metaphorically but technically. When you plant a fertile meme in my mind you literally parasitize my brain, turning it into a vehicle for the meme's propagation in just the way that a virus may parasitize the genetic mechanism of a host cell." (1976, pp. 206–207)

If Wilson's description of the brain as a machine raises doubts about the adequacy of his way of understanding the many dimensions of human consciousness and thought, which varies widely from culture to culture,

Dawkins's account of the brain as a propagator of memes should increase them many times over. Dawkins's theory of memes and how they reproduce themselves over time leaves out the possibility of reflection, insight, memory, thinking metaphorically, and meaning as having a subjective as well as culturally influenced dimensions of experience. Dawkins's radical reductionist theory of memes also fails to take account of how the above dimensions of consciousness are influenced by the taken-for-granted assumptions shared by other members of the language community. This latter point is demonstrated by the way the evolutionary fundamentalists use the industrial metaphors of their culture: brains are like machines, memes are vehicles, organisms are made up of parts that can be understood as systems that can be re-engineered.

Just as the various efforts of Christian and Islamic fundamentalists to interpret God's will make irrelevant the importance of political decision making that addresses the crisis of the world's commons, the theory of evolution becomes yet another form of fundamentalism that directs attention away from the environmental problems that are rapidly spinning out of control—that is, reaching a scale of magnitude that is beyond what can be resolved through the political process. Indeed, we may have already reached that point. The current and future demands now exceed the availability of fresh water in many regions of the world; and the self-renewing capacity of the ocean's ecosystems is similarly in doubt. And who can predict accurately what the long-term effects of the thousands and thousands of chemicals that have been released into the environment will be on humans and other species? That the United States government now alters the reports of scientists on the status of natural systems, such as global warming, in order to avoid alienating corporate supporters, suggests that the political process is unable to subordinate economic interests to the larger interest of achieving a sustainable future. If the evolutionary fundamentalists are correct in their interpretation of Nature's design process, then the monetizing of the democratic process is as irrelevant as the practice of democracy that is local and involves full participation by the community. To paraphrase Kevin Kelly's reference to how Nature has forced past technological developments to meet the test of Darwinian fitness, "Nature's agenda is out of our control" (1994, p. 471).

Western science is far more than what is represented by the evolutionary fundamentalists. Yet even its more constructive contributions, as well as the great many scientists whose efforts do not cross over into the domain of scientism, have contributed to degrading the world's ecosystems and in spreading the Western approach to development. Without science there would not have been an industrial revolution in the West, and without the recent achievements of science there would be no global communication network that enables corporations to outsource their production facilities and to spread the secular gospel of a consumer lifestyle. Science, contrary to Sagan's and Wilson's way of equating it only with the promises of the Enlightenment, has a Janus face. That is, it has made many contributions to our understanding of the life-forming and life-destructive processes, as well as contributed to longer and healthier lives for a certain segment of the world's population. But its past and current contributions to the culture-transforming industrial revolution that is spreading around the world, including the chemicals it has introduced into natural systems, represent the face of science that Sagan and Wilson overlook in order to promote its global acceptance as the one true approach to knowledge. Given the destructive side of science and the privileged role it has in Western universities, the question posed earlier about how universities contribute to undermining the commons of the world's cultures needs to be asked again. More specifically, will the current education of the next generation of scientists, including the young scientists who will graduate from Western universities and return to their own Third World cultures, enable them to recognize the importance of revitalizing the commons in ways that address eco- justice issues? Will they be aware of the limits of science, and thus avoid turning science into an ideology that justifies the actions of the already rich and powerful? Will they be able to recognize other cultural approaches to scientific knowledge—that is, a more place-based, intergenerationally connected body of knowledge of how to live within the limits and possibility of the local ecosystems? Or will their education leave them with the same hubris that characterizes the thinking of important scientists such as Wilson, Crick, Hawking, and Dawkins?

As these questions are not being widely considered within the scientific community, we face the same double bind that exists within philosophy and other academic departments that continue to perpetuate the cultural assumptions about the nature of the autonomous individual, the linear nature of progress, and an anthropocentric world that can be brought under the control of rational thought. Successful educational reforms, as we have learned from past experience, have to come from within the discipline or field of inquiry, as they are short lived and only partially successful if they are imposed by outside forces. But who is willing to jeopardize her/his career by asking the fundamental questions about the knowledge systems that control how the past is understood, and the prospects for the future? Environmentally oriented courses in the sciences and other disciplines are well intended and introduce students to important understandings, but few go far enough in clarifying how the cultural assumptions underlying the industrial culture are contributing to the spread of poverty in Third World countries and to accelerating the rate at which the ecosystems are being undermined. If we survey what educational reformers are proposing, we see that nearly all of them never come to grips with these basic issues. Rather their proposals for reform, in most instances, are based on the same assumptions that need to be questioned.

EDUCATIONAL REFORM PROPOSALS THAT REPRODUCE PRE-ECOLOGICAL WAYS OF THINKING

The Western myth that represents rationality as an attribute of the autonomous individual continues to limit our ability to understand the cultural nature of intelligence. That intelligence can also be understood as part of a larger ecological system that involves plants, animals, and other natural phenomena is an even more remote possibility. Educational reformers representing supposedly different ideological orientations share the same fundamental misconceptions that characterize the thinking of Western philosophers and the scientists who have strayed into the quagmire of futuristic prediction. The myth that equates rationality with individual autonomy (and now, with the individual's powers of self-creation) can be traced back to the non-culturally informed writings of Plato. And the myth has been renewed by philosophers of different epistemological persuasions: Rene Descartes, John Locke, and John Dewey. Richard Rorty is simply the latest in this line of ethnocentric thinking that philosophers have misrepresented as rational thought. The myth has served a number of important functions, such as providing a rationale for representing knowledge (and now data and information) as objective. It has also provided an agreed upon supposedly culturally free bedrock for assessing the students' *own* ideas. The protocol dictated by the myth of individual rationality requires students to acknowledge ideas and data they have derived from other sources—otherwise they can be charged with plagiarism. The myth has also served larger, more imperialistic, purposes, such as providing a justification for bringing Western Enlightenment thinking to cultures still mired in a demon-haunted world—to recall again Sagan's way of characterizing non-scientifically based cultures.

The myth of the rationally autonomous individual, however, is largely responsible for the inability of Western faculty and students to recognize that finding the answers to the questions posed at the beginning of this chapter is essential to reconnecting with the pathway that most cultures had taken before the processes of enclosure overwhelmed them and the natural systems—all in the name of progress. As I have pointed out in previous books (1995, 1997, 2000, 2001, 2003), a culture's way of knowing, which is based on its deepest taken-for-granted assumptions, is encoded in its multiple languaging processes—in the spoken and written word, its architecture and other expressions of material culture, and in its forms of play and aesthetic expression. Thus, to learn the languages of one's culture involves learning to think in ways that are influenced by the taken-for-granted assumptions of the culture. In earlier writings I described these cultural assumptions as root metaphors that serve as the meta-cognitive frameworks of understanding. The language that reproduces these deep patterns of interpretation carries forward the cultural group's understanding of relationships, and the attributes of the participants in the relationships. That is, learning the language also involves learning the culture's moral codes that govern relationships and how the attributes of the participants are understood. The root metaphor of patriarchy leads to a complex pattern of relationships, and a moral code that sanctioned treating women as inferior. Similarly, the root metaphor of anthropocentrism leads to viewing the environment as a resource—which means it is moral to exploit it to the fullest. And the root metaphor of progress leads to recognizing all technological innovations, regardless of the traditions they undermine, as the expression of moral behavior.

Examples of how cultural languages carry forward earlier patterns of thinking (interpretative frameworks) that will influence thinking, as well as what will be ignored, can be seen in how the root metaphor of mechanism continues to influence the thinking of Wilson, Dawkins, Crick, and Kurzweil. These supposedly cutting-edge thinkers are, in fact, reproducing an over-400-year-old pattern of thinking that can be traced back to Newton and Kepler, who understood the universe as a machine that could be observed, measured, and experimented with. The mechanism root metaphor brings into focus what can be observed, while putting out of focus, when applied to humans, the intersubjective dimensions of experience which cannot be directly observed. And when the mechanism root metaphor is applied to animals, it leads to treating them as objects of experimentation—and in the area of agriculture, it leads to an industrial approach that requires calculating production costs in relationship to profits (but ignores the long-term damage to local ecosystems). As the thinking of Wilson, Dawkins, and the other futurist scientists shows, there are a number of root metaphors that complement each other in ways that strengthen a particular way of thinking. For example, they all share the assumption that change is a linear form of progress even though there is no linear progress in the process of natural selection. They all share the same taken-for-granted assumption that the individual and, now, the gene is the basic unit of survival. Actually, Wilson and Dawkins want to have it both ways: the individual who adopts the scientific way of knowing is, according to their way of thinking, free of the influence of the cultural assumptions encoded in the metaphorical language they rely upon, such as referring to humans as machines and the brain as a problem in engineering. At the same time they hold that the scientist is an objective observer and thinker. But the bottom line is that the genes that create the brains of scientists must meet the test of Darwinian fitness. The meta-cognitive schemata they take for granted marginalize the significance of other cultural ways of knowing, and in doing so lead to the prescription that the way of knowing of Western scientists should become the model for the entire world. In effect, their evolutionary fundamentalism makes the project of Western colonization a moral act that has been 'hardwired" by thousands of years of natural selection.

While Wilson has spoken out forcefully about the danger of destroying the habitats that species depend upon, and has suggested (but given no creditable scientific evidence) that humans are genetically programmed for biophilia, his main culturally influenced pattern of thinking promotes the industrial culture that has been undermining the commons for hundreds of years. The other scientists who are promoting scientism are also contributing to an agenda that will further transform what remains of the commons into market relationships. Unfortunately, the proposals for educational reform being made by misnamed conservatives such as Mortimer Adler and William Bennett, as well as the reform proposals being made by people in the Dewey/Freire tradition of emancipatory thinking, are based on the same deep cultural assumptions that underlie the thinking of Western scientists and philosophers. While educational reformers in the Dewey/Freire tradition of thinking are critical of industrial culture, including the way in which life processes are reduced to fit the mechanistic model, they nevertheless think of change as linear and progressive, the individual or social group as engaged in the continual process of reconstructing intergenerational knowledge, and that there is only one cultural way of knowing—experimental inquiry for Dewey, critical reflection for Freire. Adler and Bennett promote many of the same cultural assumptions by arguing for a form of rationality that is based on the knowledge of great Western thinkers. And both Dewey and Freire share with Wilson, Dawkins, and the other techno-utopian thinkers that their way of knowing is more evolutionarily advanced than that of other cultures. The meta-cognitive schemata they take for granted lead them to represent traditions (intergenerational practices and ways of knowing) as a source of backwardness. They also lead them to ignore the connections between cultural/linguistic diversity and biodiversity. Indeed, their emphasis on reflective thinking as the source of problem solving, emancipation from oppressive traditions, and basis of direct democracy continues to privilege the anthropocentrism that has been so destructive of the commons.

There are now efforts to represent Dewey as an early environmental thinker, but they have not come to grips with the problem of reconciling Dewey's emphasis on the experimental mode of inquiry as the only valid approach to knowledge, as well as his emphasis on the need to continually reconstruct the knowledge of previous generations, with the diversity of the cultural commons—and the ways in which the commons are intergenerationally renewed. There are a few followers of Freire who are just now beginning to recognize that the ecological crisis cannot be ignored. For example, Moacir Gadotti, the director of the Instituto Paulo Freire in Brazil, is advocating an approach to educational reform that will foster a sense of *"planetary citizenship, a planetary civilization, a planetary conscience"* (2001, p. 2). The recognition that the ecological crisis should become the central focus of educational reform represents a major shift from the earlier Freirean emphasis on each generation becoming authentic human beings by using critical reflection to rename the world. But Gadotti's thinking is still heavily influenced by the same assumptions that are shared by Western scientists and philosophers. These assumptions can be seen in his inability to recognize the contradiction between a pedagogy of the earth and his idea that globalization "constitutes an unprecedented process of advancement in the history of mankind" (p. 8). His argument that education should not become "the transmission of culture from one generation to the next," but rather that education should be the "grand journey of each individual in his interior universe and in the universe that surrounds him" (p. 8) also reflects an unexamined and deeply problematic Western assumption. Again, we see here the way in which a taken-for-granted meta-cognitive interpretative framework reflects a culturally specific way of thinking—and in Gadotti's case, how it continues the pattern of extreme ethnocentrism shared by other Western reformers. To reiterate: they all maintain that we are evolving toward a global culture, that we cannot learn from traditions but rather must use our rational capacity to overturn them, and that life is an individual journey (or for Wilson and Dawkins, the life-struggle of genes to reproduce themselves over as many generations as possible).

The most recent conceptual distemper that is being promoted as the basis of educational reform in Western and, at last count, 29 non-Western countries is the idea that students should construct their own knowledge. The supposedly scientific basis for this approach to educational reform is found in the writings of Jean Piaget, who combined the idea that genes determine the students' stage of cognitive development with the Western assumption that autonomy represents the highest stage of human development. This approach to educational reform, which is called "constructivism," and which also has its roots in the widely shared misconceptions about the nature of cultural traditions, is based on the same ethnocentrism that characterizes the thinking of the proponents of the Western canon, and in the thinking of Dewey and Freire—and their followers. Constructivism, while it is being represented as contributing to more democratic and individual-centered societies, is really the latest expression of the Trojan Horse of Western colonialism. What it paves the way for is not the revitalization of the commons but the transnational corporations that need the intergenerational sources of self-reliance to be replaced by the form of individualism that is dependent upon consumerism to survive.

The commons is not an abstraction, but the ongoing relationships between the cultural practices that characterize daily life and the natural systems that make life possible. Thus, the commons will vary from place to place—from the villages located in the valleys and on the slopes of the Peruvian Andes to the prairies of central Canada, to the mesas of northern Arizona, to the forests of Siberia, to the suburbs of London and San Francisco. The ecosystems vary just as the cultures dependent upon them vary widely. When we begin to think about the commons as specific ecosystems and intergenerationally connected cultural practices that may in some instances be destructive of the environment while in others are nurturing, we can recognize more easily that the mainstream theories of Western philosophers, futurist-thinking scientists, and educational reformers continue the pattern of thinking that underlies various efforts to impose a Western agenda on the rest of the world. This agenda has many sources of support: Christian fundamentalists, an industrial-dependent lifestyle, a global computer-mediated form of consciousness, and the neo-liberal ideology that continues to be misrepresented as the expression of conservatism.

In order to avoid reproducing educational reforms that are based on the industrial cultural patterns that are destroying the commons it will first be necessary to consider several examples of communities that are revitalizing their commons. Their efforts to revitalize the traditions of self-sufficiency and mutual support, to create private and public spaces that are free of commercialism, and to resist and even reverse the industrial pressures of enclosure, represent models of education that need to be replicated in future efforts to reform public schools and universities. However, before we consider the implications of the many approaches that are now being taken to the revitalization of the commons, it is important to provide a more complex way of understanding the cultural assumptions that Western thinkers have reduced to a conceptual formula. That is, we need to have a more complex understanding of such words as change and tradition. We also need a more adequate understanding of how, over the short term, the industrial culture of the West is able to defy the logic of natural selection—and over the long term put the world's cultures and natural systems at greater risk of collapse.

Misconception 1: *Thinking of change as the dominant reality and traditions as the source of oppression and backwardness*

Change is indeed an aspect of everyday experience, even in cultures where there is the assumption that certain ways of thinking and behaving should not change. There are changes in weather patterns, as well as changes that result from individualized interpretations (and misinterpretations) of cultural practices. Changes also are part of the growth of individuals as they move through the life cycle from birth to death. And few cultures, even those that wrongly assume that traditions do not change, can avoid changes rippling through the fabric of everyday life that result from the adoption of new technologies such as the computer and the cell phone. The problem with the formulaic treatment of change in the thinking of evolutionary fundamentalists, techno-futurists, and the educational reformers is that they equate change with progress. That is, they give it ontological status instead of recognizing that change is sometimes problematic in ways that are not always understood by members of the culture. They also ignore that it needs to be evaluated within the context of each culture. The abstract representation of change, as though cultural context is irrelevant, turns it into a powerful component of an ideology. And as an ideology, it undermines the need for participatory decision-making about which changes contribute to sustaining the commons.

Just as change is an inevitable aspect of daily life (which is different from progress being inevitable), traditions are also inescapable. The continuity between generations—which may range from the use of technologies, identity-forming narratives, norms governing relationships and processes of political decision-making, approaches to healing and to patterns of mutual aid, involve the re-enactment of traditions. But just as change is ever present, so is the process of modifying traditions. The modification process may be too slow for some of the members of the culture, while to others the wrongful nature of the tradition may require rejecting it entirely. As pointed out earlier, every aspect of culture that is re-enacted over three or four generations (which is the time span for a cultural practice to become taken for granted) becomes a tradition. And because it is taken for granted, such as how we address an envelope, greet a guest, and understand our civil liberties, most of a culture's traditions become so much a part of the natural attitude toward everyday life that they are not recognized as traditions. Traditions can also be understood as the replicating patterns and the sources of continuity between the past and the present. The dialectic between traditions and the process of change can be seen in the way the DNA carries forward the information that guides the development of a new generation that has similar but not identical characteristics of the previous generation. Similarly, if we examine the traditions of architecture, jazz, medicine, or airplane design we find the same process of change being largely a modification of a tradition—rather than as a complete break (which may also happen). Changes that lead to patterns that do not survive over three generations, such as the design features of clothes, cars, houses, and so on, are fads; but the basic traditions of wearing clothes, the car with an internal combustion engine and metal frame, and the structural and material nature of houses persist.

Both change and tradition are essential aspects of the commons. Change is ongoing in the cycles of natural systems, and in how the humans respond to these changes. And traditions are also essential, as they often represent the patterns of thinking, behavior, and technologies that have been refined over generations of place and community-based experience. Mentoring, patterns of moral reciprocity, reading the constant ways in which natural systems communicate their reproductive viability, approaches to ceremonies and celebrations, are all examples of traditions. As sources of empowerment and civic responsibility, it is important for the members of the culture to always be assessing what needs to be conserved as well as what needs to be changed. What is unique about the nature of industrial culture is that its promoters are primarily concerned with introducing changes in the form of new technologies and consumer goods that create new dependencies on what can be industrially produced. For example, the efforts of Monsanto to introduce what has been called the "terminator seed" that was genetically engineered to produce a sterile seed, thus forcing farmers to buy seed for the next year's planting, is a prime example of how the industrial cultural approach to change is oriented to undermining intergenerational knowledge and technologies that are the basis of relative self-sufficiency. On the other hand, the tradition of preserving seeds adapted to the local characteristics of the soil, weather conditions, and so forth, is an example of local knowledge that is the source of empowerment and thus resistance to the further enclosure of the commons. Industrial culture is also an example of a complex set of traditions, ranging from the accumulated and refined knowledge of the sciences to the technologies that also range from machines to social techniques. But they differ from the traditions of the commons by virtue of being understood and applied as though they have universal applicability. That is, they are implemented on the assumption that local cultural knowledge is either irrelevant or a source of resistance by backward people. In either case, the goal of industrial culture is to overturn local traditions in order to make the people dependent upon what can be industrially produced—and the constant stream of innovations that need to be purchased. The role of technological innovation in the cycle of dependence can be seen in the way in which it is necessary to upgrade one's computer if its many functions, and some new ones, are to be utilized.

Misconception 2: *Misinterpreting how natural selection determines the moral values that are the basis of the cultures that are better adapted*

As suggested earlier, evolution is being used by futurist scientists to explain how cultural "memes" must meet the same test of Darwinian fitness as genes. The faulty logic that underlies this use of the theory of evolution is that just as the test of better-adapted genes is that they lead to leaving more offspring, successful memes also survive and spread over many generations, while less well adapted memes become extinct. In short, the cultures that are selected by the environment to survive displace cultures that "choose badly," to use Wilson's phrase. The logic of natural selection, when used to explain which cultures survive and which do not, leads to a world monoculture—as memes (cultural patterns) of the better-adapted cultures displace the memes of more poorly adapted cultures. In a word, this logic deviates radically from how natural selection works in the natural world where the dynamics of mutation and the constant test of fitness for surviving in nature's various niches lead to greater diversity. This is the opposite of the current use of Darwinian logic to explain why scientifically based cultures are better adapted than the cultures that have developed the moral norms that protect the commons from being degraded in ways that threaten the well-being of future generations.

Explaining the origin and test of Darwinian fitness that must be met by a culture's moral values is especially problematic. A case in point is the argument of Wilson and other evolutionary fundamentalists such as Richard Alexander. Thinking of moral values as memes that survive because they have been selected by the environment distorts a fundamental reality of cultures: namely that their moral values are derived from their mythopoetic narratives and survive over generations because they are encoded in the languaging processes of the culture. The evolutionary fundamentalist position, as Richard Alexander put it, holds that "each person is programmed by the history of natural selection to maximize the likelihood of survival of his/her genetic material through reproduction and nepotism" (1987, p. 108). Wilson's statements that "the brain is a machine assembled not to understand itself, but to survive" (1998a), and that moral behavior "is urged into existence through the biases in mental development that are encoded in the genes" (1998b, p. 65) does not support his argument about the evolutionary importance of moral behavior that strengthens cooperation. What Wilson and Alexander overlook is that regardless of whether the social unit engages in cooperation or sanctions more individual-centered behavior, the bottom line is that every moral code must meet the test of survival of the fittest. Also overlooked by the evolutionary fundamentalists is that the time frame within which evolution operates may leave the question of which moral codes are the better adapted unresolved for hundreds, even thousands of years. Over the short term, the moral code of the dictator or the corporate elite will appear as the better adapted because his/their offspring are more likely to pass on their genetic material than the groups killed off or forced further into poverty.

There is another point that needs to be made in considering how evolutionary fundamentalists explain the genetic basis of cultural memes. Whether a culture views water as sacred or as a commodity that is governed by the supposed laws of supply and demand depends largely on the nature of its mythopoetic narratives. If the evolutionary fundamentalists are correct about genes being the basis of various cultural/moral predispositions, then there would have to be a gene that predisposes the people in the West to create a mythopoetic narrative that represents water as a natural resource, and another gene that predisposes the various cultures in the Indian subcontinent to create a mythopoetic narrative that represents water as sacred—with access to water being a basic human right. Clearly, there is no way science can provide evidence for the claim that genes predispose people toward different cultural practices and beliefs. However, the more important reason for not relying upon evolutionary fundamentalism for guidance in thinking about the values that are essential to revitalizing the commons is that humans do not have to take responsibility for their moral behavior. As Wilson put it, it is the "environment (that) ultimately selects which genes will do the prescribing (1998a, p. 137).

These criticisms of evolutionary fundamentalism should not be interpreted to mean that there is no relationship between the changes occurring in local environments and the survivability of a culture. Indeed, the ability of a culture to adapt its practices to fit what is sustainable within its environmental niche (or bioregion) is critical to its survival—and to the survival of neighboring cultures. When the values and practices of a culture exceed what can be sustained locally, and it turns to exploiting the resources and markets of other countries, it may ensure its own survival over the short term—but put both itself and the exploited countries at greater risk—in terms of contributing to social unrest, contributing to unemployment, contaminating local environments, and disrupting the intergenerational patterns of mutual support. A current example of a culture that is ignoring the importance of adapting its practices and values to the limits and possibilities of its own bioregions can be seen in how the North American Free Trade Agreement allows American agribusiness to export corn to Mexico at a price that cannot be matched by the local Mexican farmers who have relied upon the growing of corn on small plots of land for hundreds of years. In addition to other modern pressures, the enclosure of their commons by the industrial approach to agriculture is forcing Mexican farmers to leave their ancestral land and a subsistence lifestyle for the even greater economic uncertainties of urban existence. There are other consequences that will undermine the future prospects of our own culture. For example, the use of chemicals to produce the massive crops that are marketed at a price that undercuts local producers here and in other cultures has a destructive impact on the groundwater and micro-organisms that are essential for the long-term fertility of the soil. Thus the commons of the seemingly Darwinian fittest culture is further undermined. And somewhere in the years ahead, the environment will cease to support the practices and values that are driven more by an outmoded ideology than by an awareness of how local ecosystems reproduce themselves on a sustainable basis.

In short, evolution entails a moral ethic that is at the center of various efforts to revitalize the commons. However, it needs to be understood in a profoundly different way than is represented in the writings of Wilson and Alexander. Gregory Bateson summarized this ethic when he wrote that "the unit of survival is organism plus environment. We are learning by bitter experience that the organism which destroys its environment destroys itself." He concludes with the observation that "the unit of evolutionary survival turns out to be identical with the unit of mind" (1972, p. 483). Here he is using "mind" as synonymous with the thought patterns and values of a culture, plus the information exchanges between the different elements that constitute the ecosystem. To sum up, while the explanation cannot be scientifically proven that the environment selects the genes and thus cultural memes that will survive, the interdependent relationship between culture and environment needs to be kept foremost in mind. The critical issue is not to interpret the Darwinian fitness of a culture on the basis of the reproductive success of its memes over generations to come and its ability to subjugate or overturn the memes of other cultures. Rather, it is the ability of a culture to live within the sustainable limits of its local environment. Thus, the challenge becomes a matter of focusing on the revitalization of the commons and not on colonizing other cultures in ways that destroy their commons.

The commons can also be understood as an ecology; more specifically, as a cultural ecology that interacts with the ecology of natural systems. The original Greek understanding of "oikos" meant the management of the household—which included the ongoing human relationships and activities within the larger context of the life-sustaining natural systems. Understanding the commons as an ecology requires a different moral framework than what is emphasized in the West where moral values are supposed to be a matter of individual judgment. The view that moral values are individually chosen is problematic for a number of reasons. In addition to the way in which language carries forward the moral templates of the cultures, which we have already discussed, the emphasis on the perspective of the individual has reduced awareness of the multiple relationships that are an integral part of every experience. These relationships—which range from the air we breathe, the sounds of nearby birds, and the rustle of the leaves on the trees to walking past a stranger, standing in a line, greeting a neighbor, responding to a call for assistance, and so forth—are part of the larger moral ecology. These relationships can also be understood as everything where a difference which makes a difference, to use Bateson's phrase, leads to some form of response. Whether we are aware of it or not, our responses to differences—in someone's tone of voice, in the thoughtful behavior of another driver, in the taste of industrially prepared food, in the smog that obstructs vision and makes breathing more difficult, and so on—are moral responses. That is, when the day is filled with relationships that involve trying to sell something to others, in making repairs, or in walking across a field, moral judgments are constantly involved—even when we are not being morally reflective. We may think that we are simply working or in the role of a customer, but if the response is characterized by silence and acquiescence in the face of shoddy goods and indifference to the quality of the workmanship, we are in essence giving our approval to it as a moral norm.

Understanding the commons (both the human and natural systems) as a moral ecology requires a different language than that which starts with a reference to the personal perspective, such as "I see," "I want," " I think," and so forth. As Bateson pointed out, when it is assumed that the individual's unique and supposedly culturally uninfluenced perspective is made the primary reference point, and thus the source of judgment of the relationships that will be given attention, the other relationships that are part of the experience are not seen. In effect, language both illuminates and hides. This means that the language that will enable us to move beyond the moral reductionism and relativism of individual judgment needs to take account of the many activities and relationships that are part of the commons—as well as the activities and relationships that support the further enclosure of the commons. This language is developed through understanding the layered nature of natural systems, from the living systems that revitalize the soil, the nature of energy exchanges between plants, animals, and humans, the cycles that renew the sources of fresh water, to the only slightly less complex relationships and sources of interdependence that we call culture.

Being explicitly aware of the traditions we rely upon—legal systems, nature and uses of different technologies (social and mechanical), narratives, ceremonies, ways of preparing and sharing a meal, injustices that have been overcome, eco-justice issues that have not yet been fully addressed, the past mistreatment and exploitation of others, the systems of mutual aid, and patterns of moral reciprocity—is part of the ecology of the commons that we need to be able to name if we are to recognize what needs to be supported and renewed in ways that enhance the possibilities of future generations. We also need to be able to name the ideas, values, forms of relationships, and activities that endanger what remains of the commons. Again, there is a connection between awareness and having the vocabulary and explanatory framework that is necessary for challenging what may enrich the few at the expense of the common good. Without the language necessary for making explicit the different aspects of the commons, there can be no communicative competence—and thus no democratic process. In order to test the adequacy of this generalization, I invite the reader to ask friends, students, family, people who work behind the counter or in the office, even teachers and university professors, if they can explain the ways in which the World Trade Organization operates, its influence on environmental legislation, its impact on the economies of Third World cultures, and whether it contributes to more democratic societies. The silence that will follow the asking of any part of this question will quickly lead, as I have found, to changing the focus of the conversation.

The challenge now is to develop the vocabulary necessary for exercising communicative competence in challenging the ways in which the commons continues to be enclosed, as well as in affirming what contributes to a better balance between the non-monetized patterns of life within the commons and the industrial culture that now provides the infrastructure and service we now seem dependent upon. As the commons, and the nature of the industrial forces that are undermining what remains of the commons, vary from bioregion to bioregion, we cannot start with the vocabularies that have their origins in abstract educational or social theories. Nor should we rely upon the vocabularies that represent a supposedly universal understanding of the good, the just, and the true. We must start, instead, with the vocabulary that is grounded in the multiple dimensions of life within the commons—which, as was pointed out earlier, are always place-based, rooted in specific traditions of intergenerational knowledge that can often be traced back to powerful and taken-for-granted mythopoetic narratives. Considering different approaches to the revitalization of the commons will, I believe, lead to seeing common characteristics in approaches to revitalizing the commons, as well as in resisting the forces of enclosure. And these commons approaches to affirmation and resistance will provide the basis for discussing the educational reforms that now need to be considered.

Chapter Three

Revitalizing the Commons of the African-American Communities in Detroit

With Rebecca Martusewicz

The commons are as varied in North America as are the differences in natural systems and in the traditions of cultural groups that inhabit them. The natural systems that stretch across southern Saskatchewan and northwest Montana and North Dakota are vastly different from the natural systems of the Pacific Northwest. And these natural systems, which vary widely within the boundaries of each of these geographical and political units, are vastly different from those found in the American southwest and the Canadian Maritimes. While people in these different regions may speak the same language (which again reflect regional differences) and identify with a common set of political symbols, they nevertheless often think in ways that reflect their historical cultural roots as well as their experience with the natural systems their lives have depended upon—often over many generations. The Cajun Americans of Louisiana, for example, have different expectations about weather patterns, fish and other animals, and the sources of potable water than the indigenous people living along the coast of Alaska. And even the taken-for-granted expectations of the inhabitants of two states that seem so similar, Oregon and Vermont, are profoundly different—especially the experience of the commons during the winter.

Wallace Stegner writes about being rooted in a place—or what we are referring to as the environmental commons. Reflecting upon his own early years of rootlessness, and his own maturing sensitivity to what transforms a piece of ground and human interactions into a community, he writes that

a place is not a place until people have been born in it, have grown up in it, lived in it, known it, died in it—have both experienced and shaped it, as individuals, families, neighborhoods, and communities, over more than one generation. Some are born in their place, some find it, some realize after

long searching that the place they left is the one they have been searching
for. But whatever their relation to it, it is made a place only by slow accrual,
like a coral reef. (1992: 201)

Differences in cultural ways of knowing, including the prejudices, fears, and
poverty of a group, may alter the meaning that place has for them. These differences may even influence whether they experience place as a dynamic set
of nurturing relationships, as is the case of the Quechua of the Peruvian
Andes and even in rural and urban areas of North America, as an opportunity for amassing wealth as many of the early Euro-Americans experienced
it, or as a temporary resting place before moving on in a vaguely defined
quest for getting ahead. Putting down roots, as Stegner points out, is an
intergenerational experience whereby place and self-identity, even in the
most barren environment, merge in a way that gives rise to a sense of being
a responsible citizen of the commons.

Today, the diversity of the commons and the cultural beliefs and
practices that influence whether the life-supporting natural systems are
exploited or nurtured are being threatened by the spread of the industrial
culture that began in the Midlands of England just over two hundred years
ago. The industrial culture, with its emphasis on transforming more aspects
of these diverse human and natural systems that constitute the commons
into market relationships, has as its primary goal the creation of a world
monoculture—where tastes, clothes, technologies, ways of understanding
social relationships, and the purpose in life can be met through what can be
mass-produced and consumed. This emphasis on bigness and the centralization of power—in the scale of production, in the size of government, in
the relentless drive to increase profits, in the universal application of a guiding ideology and approach to education—is now being justified on the
grounds that it meets the test of Darwinian fitness. But it does not fit the
micro-scale at which the life-regenerating processes of natural systems sustain the diversity of species. Nor does it fit the daily patterns of face-to-face
human interactions that are the sources of meaning, daily negotiation of
relationships and responsibilities, and the need for work that provides for
self-expression as well as for food and shelter.

The emphasis of the industrial culture on bigness and sameness now
requires that the different cultures of the world become increasingly
dependent upon a money economy for meeting needs that were previously
not recognized as needs, and to abandon meeting genuine needs through

traditional networks of support and barter. The double bind inherent in this emphasis on mass production and consumption is that the local community-centered networks, the work that is relevant to the needs of the community, and the mutual exchange systems are being undermined. Mass production, in effect, makes the skills of the people irrelevant to their ability to earn a living. And in not being able to find work, the people lack the money necessary for purchasing what is being produced by an increasingly automated and worker-free technology.

In addressing the problem of how to revitalize the commons, it is necessary to avoid the trap of assuming that there is one best approach—one set of ideas that can be universally applied. Educators who are focused on social reform, particularly in achieving social justice for all, make this mistake when they assume that their language of emancipation has universal applicability. That is, the words that are to guide their efforts in achieving social justice—freedom, emancipation, progress, individualism, autonomy, and even democracy—take on different meanings for cultural groups that do not share the Western assumptions that these educational reformers take for granted. The irony is that these words, and the cultural assumptions they encode when used by Western reformers, may become the unintended Trojan Horse that continues the Western project of colonizing other cultures—thus undermining the traditions of place-based knowledge that contribute to the viability of the commons.

Stegner's observation about the importance of place-based intergenerational roots, even in a physical environment that has been ravaged by years of industrial exploitation, helps to understand the motivation and energy that lies behind the efforts of the African-American community in Detroit to revitalize its commons. And the efforts of this community are a testament to the fact that even the poorest of the urban poor can envision an alternative future—and can mobilize the community in a way that leads to less reliance on the industrial culture that is failing so many groups. Their approach to revitalizing the commons also stands in sharp contrast to how educational reformers envision the achievement of social justice. We shall return to this problem later in the chapter. For now, it is necessary to provide an overview of the conditions that have led the leadership within the African-American communities of Detroit's east side, the Northwest Goldberg neighborhood, and in Old Redford to envision an alternative, postindustrial future. What stands out is how the community leaders understand the importance of local democracy to making the recovery of the natural environment the basis of moving toward greater self-sufficiency as a community. Economic issues remain an important concern, but their approach to revitalizing the commons involves a more complex understanding of community, including how participation in community projects represents an alternative to the industrial culture's narrowing of human purpose to what Adam Smith referred to as the human propensity to "truck, barter, and trade."

While the history of African Americans in Detroit can be traced back to before the Civil War, it was the growth of the auto industry in the 1920s and 1930s that sparked the migration of African Americans from the south as well as other ethnic groups from Europe. Hungarian, Polish, English, Scottish, and Jewish neighborhoods, along with the recently arrived African Americans, created a rich patchwork of neighborhoods that were, especially for the African Americans, sources of racial conflict and prejudice. From early on, discrimination effectively shut the African Americans out of the higher paying and skill-based jobs in the auto industry, leaving them with the low paying and low-status jobs as janitors, dishwashers, domestic servants, and the most hazardous and dirty factory jobs. Following World War II, the employment opportunities in metropolitan Detroit, which had swelled from 857,000 in 1940 to 1,119,000 in 1950, started to decline rapidly as manufacturing plants were moved to the suburbs. This trend, which continues today, further undermined the ability of African Americans to find well-paid jobs (and increasingly any jobs at all) even when they possessed the skills and requisite educational background.

The history of the African-American community in Detroit also includes discrimination in the areas of education, housing, access to adequate transportation, police protection, and public services that Euro-Americans who had not fled to the suburbs could take for granted. As the manufacturing plants were moved to the suburbs, the city failed to provide the bus system that would have enabled African Americans to travel to where the job opportunities existed. While working class whites who were economically barred from the more expensive suburban homes could at least find decent housing closer to work cites, African Americans were systematically excluded from housing in white neighborhoods in the city as well as the newly developing suburban areas through a practice known as redlining by banks and real estate companies. A city police force that had a long history of using excessive violence against members of the African-American community was another expression of the racially divided city. Racial riots, which occurred as far back as the Civil War, were also a periodic feature of life.

Today, in spite of the achievements of Coleman Young, the former African-American mayor of Detroit, little has changed for the African-American community—except that it now represents the largest group living in metropolitan Detroit. With the change in demographics, where in 1990 only 10 percent of the population were white, and the loss of tax revenues as the manufacturing plants moved to the suburbs, the economic resources of the city rapidly declined. But this decline did not prevent the city from constructing new stadiums for the professional baseball and football teams. The allocation of the diminished resources for public services, including support for public schools, continues to be influenced by the discriminatory practices of the white bureaucrats and politicians.

Driving through the African-American neighborhoods today is, in places, like driving through the remains of a war zone. Vacant lots are overgrown with grass and filled with discarded industrial equipment. Abandoned cars serve as makeshift shelters, and in some areas the vacant lots give way to open fields that are being reinhabited by wild animals and bird populations (notably coyotes and pheasants) not usually associated with an urban area. Children playing in the vacant lots continue to be exposed to the possibility of lead poisoning, and to the damaging effects of the other toxic chemicals left as a legacy of the golden era of auto production—and by plants that continue to engage in the incineration of toxic waste material without regard for the safety of nearby schools and playgrounds. Houses are in various stages of disrepair, with an occasional house being partly or completely burned down—which can only be explained as being the result of deliberate arson. There are still drug traffickers, but most of the population is a mix of grandparents, children, and single mothers. With few opportunities for employment, the generation that represents the working years is largely absent.

Also visible are the hard realities of poverty and limited opportunities that are the result of years of systemic discrimination. According to the statistics of the U.S. Census Bureau for the year 2000, the level of education within the African-American community ranged from 32 percent having completed high school to 1.4 percent having achieved a graduate or professional degree. The lack of employment opportunities has resulted in 55 percent of the grandparents being the primary caregivers of children. Household incomes also reflect a degree of poverty not found in other regions of the country. For example, 39 percent of households have an income of less than $10,000 a year, with 11.7 percent having incomes between $10,000 and $15,000 per year. The number of households with an income above $35,000 falls off dramatically. A final figure that helps put in perspective the challenges faced by the community leaders working to revitalize the commons is that 30 percent of the households with children under 18 years of age have no biological father present.

In spite of these manifestations of the ongoing and systemic-based poverty, the various efforts to revitalize the commons have many supporters within the community. One source of community activism is a group called the Concerned Citizens of Northwest Goldberg, which is led by Juanita Newton, Charles Simmons, and Brenda Smith. In addition to the activism of the citizens of Brush Park, the James and Grace Lee Boggs Center (whose former director was Jim Embry) stands out as a leader in grassroots community renewal. All of these groups come together under the umbrella of an organization co-chaired by Simmons, Smith, and Elena Herrada called the Committee for the Political Resurrection of Detroit (CPR), which decided to focus its efforts on the Northwest Goldberg neighborhood in 2002–2003. Members of the Boggs Center also joined this work. These groups are demonstrating that building networks of community support is essential to revitalizing the commons—including the aspect of the commons that can be called the human spirit.

The revitalization projects promoted by the Northwest Goldberg activists include both the beautification of important institutions within the community (planting flowers around the Duffield Library and the local police station) and fostering community participation in clearing former industrial sites of the discarded rusty machinery so the land can be used for community gardens and playgrounds for children. Workshops are also held for parents (mostly grandparents) on how to deal with the legacy of lead contamination, both in the soil where children play and in the painted walls of houses. A small group of local high school youth take leadership roles in this work in an organization called Lead Busters.

The community gardens are an especially powerful model of the participatory, intergenerationally connected nature of revitalizing the commons, demonstrating how this work differs from the industrial approach to the production and processing of food. Children and adults make decisions about which overgrown, debris-filled lots will be cleared, as well as about what will be planted. This local, on-the-ground expression of democracy also includes decisions about how adults and children will be involved in the ongoing task of maintaining the gardens, and how to use art produced primarily by young children in the form of painted rocks cleared from the lot, to claim the land for the neighborhood and discourage illegal dumping by construction companies. Unlike the industrial approach to the production of food where the members of the community have to participate in the money economy in order to be able to purchase food, the harvest from the community gardens is freely distributed to the members of the community.

In effect, the gardens are centers of community activity that foster a different set of values that are especially important to the younger members of the community: cooperation, learning how to nurture natural processes, acquiring the knowledge and skills that can be used to achieve greater self-sufficiency, developing good eating habits that contrast with the diet of industrially prepared food, taking responsibility for the success of a community-centered activity, and learning from the community's master gardener who carries forward what has been learned from previous generations about the complex ecology that governs the cycle of planting seeds, nurturing the growth of different plants, and eating food that is not dependent upon a petroleum based approach to agriculture.

The community gardens are a source of powerful educational experiences that reinforce the form of citizenship essential to strengthening the commons. While at work hauling away debris from an overgrown field, or working the soil in a newly tilled garden site, adults tell each other stories and exchange knowledge of earlier days when southern relatives made their livings on farms, or about a nearby church where Malcolm X once inspired them, or an empty lot where a neighborhood school once stood. What both adults and children learn via ongoing intergenerational exchange stands in sharp contrast to the values and ways of thinking fostered by participation in the industrial culture, which include the pursuit of individual self-interest, competition, indifference to the social value of what is being produced, and ignoring the environmentally destructive impact of consumer items that range from SUVs and computers to the excessive packaging of nearly every consumer item.

Unfortunately, the power of the media, the individually centered and industrially oriented nature of the school curriculum, and the constant encounter with peers who have been indoctrinated with the values that equate social status with brand-name consumerism, compete with the values and ways of thinking reinforced by participating in the community gardens. In too many instances, the influence of industrial culture has the effect of marginalizing the experience of gardening or storytelling as being special, but not part of the mainstream of daily life.

Just as the importance of the gardens is constantly being marginalized by the multiple messages of industrial culture that equate consumerism as the sign of a successful life and the source of happiness, the other activities of the Northwest Goldberg community have come under similar pressure. The continuation of these activities is thus a source of resistance to these pressures. At the same time, they affirm the value of the commons. Among these activities is the summer program sponsored by the Duffield Library that includes community picnics, tutoring, mentoring, and games that range from chess matches to checkers and dominoes. These activities not only strengthen social relationships, they also serve as examples of activities that do not further discriminate against the poor by requiring money in order to participate. Mentoring that develops latent skills and talents, which may range from playing an instrument to building a piece of furniture, does not require the payment of a fee. While the importance of mentoring is generally overlooked within the industrial culture because it does not contribute to the gross domestic product that can be measured and taxed, its significance to the revitalization of the commons must be judged on other grounds. What is genuinely important is that mentoring is governed by the same ethos found in an indigenous culture where the code of reciprocity dictates that work be returned rather than paid. In the case of mentoring, the relationship may be passed along, as the mentored becomes the mentor to the members of the next generation.

The range of non-consumer dependent activities held at the Duffield Library may lack the high-status visibility of media-promoted activities, such as a professional football or basketball game, but they are nevertheless examples of community self-sufficiency. Viewed within the larger context of the ecologically and culturally destructive impact of the industrial culture that is now being spread around the world, these community-enhancing activities represent expressions of resistance. To paraphrase E. F. Schumacher, they demonstrate that small is not only beautiful—it is also the source of humanity's future survival.

The revitalization efforts of the Northwest Goldberg community activists do not stand alone. The systemic sources of poverty—poor public services, lack of employment opportunities, inadequate public transportation, lack of culturally sensitive policing, the redlining on the part of banks and insurance companies, and so forth—are also the focus of the

Northwest Goldberg community activists. In effect, the revitalization of the commons requires that the long-standing discriminatory practices that characterize the history of Detroit politics also be addressed. Juanita Newton, for example, serves as chairperson of the committee that is attempting to save funding for libraries and to keep them as public institutions. She is also a member of the 3rd Police Precinct Community Relations Council, a precinct delegate to the State of Michigan Democratic Party, and a certified social worker and teacher. Drawing on her experience as a 4-H Club leader, she works closely with teachers in one particular neighborhood school to teach special needs students basic horticultural skills.

Charles Simmons, in addition to being a professor at Eastern Michigan University, is co-chair of the Committee for the Political Resurrection of Detroit (CPR) which has as its main agenda the development of a grassroots movement that will work for neighborhood empowerment and community control of schools, police, community health, and decisions about land use. Citing staggering statistics about asthma rates among young children and the elderly in the area, the group successfully led the fight to close down the Henry Ford Hospital incinerator. Other demands of the CPR include achieving a moratorium on the privatization of all city agencies and services—such as the municipal water system. In addition to demanding that all workers receive a living wage when working for the city, the CPR has run its own slate of candidates in citywide elections. Newton and Simmons, along with CPR co-chairs and labor activists Elena Herrada and Brenda Smith, are among many activists within the African-American community who understand that revitalizing their neighborhoods, including the natural systems they depend upon, requires participating in the wider geopolitical decision-making processes that impact their lives at the local level. In effect, they model how revitalizing the commons of local neighborhoods requires revitalizing the surrounding commons, and challenging the system of beliefs and values that have put these surrounding commons on a self-destructive pathway.

The revitalization of the commons is also the mission of the James and Grace Lee Boggs Center for the Nurturance of Community Leadership. Rooted in over forty years of grassroots activism by the late James Boggs (1919–1993) and his wife Grace Lee, and officially founded in 1995 by friends and supporters of the couple, the center has become the seedbed for ideas of how to transform Detroit into a postindustrial society. Providing the meeting place for current and future leaders to formulate and

debate the ideas that will guide future revitalization projects is only part of
the center's mission. Its other activities have a more immediate impact on
the African-American community. In effect, the Boggs Center continues
the lifelong efforts of James and Grace Lee Boggs to work for social justice and peace issues in the Detroit area. An African American born and
raised in Alabama, James Boggs was a lifelong Detroit auto worker, labor
organizer, and writer. Grace Lee, born to Chinese immigrant parents and
holder of a Ph.D. in philosophy from Bryn Mawr College, married James
Boggs in 1953. Together they helped to organize protests, wrote books on
the need for revolutionary social change, and were at the center of community activism for over four decades.

Grace Lee Boggs is still involved in community building, and in writing
a weekly column for the local African-American newspaper, *The Michigan
Citizen*. But the center, until recently guided by Jim Embry, a Kentucky
native, carries on the tradition of emphasizing that democratic social change
depends upon combining grassroots activism with a vision of what contributes to the self-sufficiency of the community. Conceptualizing an alternative future for Detroit has been the main focus of local and international
conferences held at the Boggs Center. The overall plan for transforming
Detroit, which is called Adamah, emerged from these conferences, and from
collaboration with the University of Detroit Mercy School of Architecture,
urban designer Kyong Park, and local residents. The Hebrew meaning of
Adamah, "of the earth," is central to the community's plan for its own self-
reliant future. Instead of using Detroit's years as an industrial leader as the
model for the future, the Adamah plan is based on understanding the characteristics of the bioregion before it was altered by humans—first by indigenous cultures and later by the French who displaced them. Understanding
the location of trails, farms, and roads of these earlier inhabitants, as well the
flow of streams and other environmental characteristics, provides the basic
framework for how the Adamah project would go about regenerating the
land, thus making urban agriculture the future basis of self-sufficiency.

But the Adamah vision involves more than combining urban agriculture
with a decentralized approach to education, economic activity, politics, and
other cultural activities. The two and a half square miles east of downtown
Detroit that is to be revitalized is also to be based on ecologically informed
approaches to providing the people with their own sources of energy. The
plan calls for fields of corn that can be transformed into ethanol, as well as
windmills that can provide the electrical power needed by the community.

In addition, Adamah is to have its own air and water purification systems, local markets that facilitate the non-monetized exchange of goods and services, and a combination of single-family homes as well as co-housing neighborhoods that have their own gardens. While the Adamah plan for the future envisions a return to the local place-based community that characterized earlier settlements, its approach to local democratic decision-making, economic interdependence, and place-based education will incorporate the new energy-efficient technologies and understandings of how natural systems renew themselves. In effect, the culture is to be organized in ways that complement the workings of natural systems, rather than exploiting them.

While the plan is still a blueprint for achieving a postindustrial future, it has been transformed into "Sustainable Detroit," which is a group that serves as a sort of networking clearinghouse for grassroots activities and revitalization efforts. However, the on-the-ground community revitalization programs sponsored by the Boggs Center, in conjunction with other groups, represent the first steps in transforming the plan into a reality. These include the Arts and Children Creating Community Together (AC3T) program that fosters a sense of pride in using the arts to beautify community buildings such as public schools. In other art projects, a Boggs Center–sponsored program called Detroit Summer works with local artists and children during off-school months to paint huge murals on the sides of other buildings to represent the Detroit they would like to see. These art projects are often done in conjunction and proximity with community gardening projects as well where students learn to till, plant, and care for flowers as well as food.

Detroit Summer continues the tradition and supports a renewal of the Freedom Schools that began with the civil rights movement. The primary purpose of the school is to provide African-American youth the opportunity to reflect on the structures of power that are responsible for the community's continued impoverishment. In Grace Lee Boggs's words, "we need a movement to challenge the concept of schools as mainly training centers for jobs in the corporate structure, or for individual upward mobility and replace it with the concept of schools as places where children learn firsthand the skills of democracy and the responsibilities of citizenship and self-government." The Freedom School brings together teachers, university professors, parents, students, and community activists for the purpose of clarifying strategies of empowerment and the achievement of greater self-reliance as a community.

Other activities sponsored by the Boggs Center include the Back Alley Bikes shop, the Power of Ideas Book Club, and the Gardening Angels. The Back Alley Bike shop provides a place where the youth of the community can repair or build their own bikes from recycled parts, thus teaching the importance of learning skills of self-reliance. In addition, it helps the youth of the community to be less dependent upon the money economy both in terms of having to purchase a bicycle and in paying a bus fare. The Power of Ideas Book Club meets another objective of the Boggs Center, which is the promotion of dialogue about ideas that the members of the club want to explore further. The members of the club suggest the title of the books they want to make the focal point of their discussions. Again, it's a community-building activity with little or no adverse impact on the environment. The Gardening Angels are another example of the bootstrap economics that relies upon the knowledge of the largely southern-born African-American elders who plant flowers around the community and maintain the vegetable gardens. The elders are master gardeners who are passing their knowledge and experience on to the younger members of the community. Together, they have cleared overgrown and debris-filled vacant lots, turning them into gardens whose fresh vegetable are distributed to the members of the community.

These activities are consistent with the Boggs Center's vision of creating a postindustrial community where self-sufficiency, the use of ecologically informed technologies, a mix of barter and a money economy, and an intergenerationally connected community serve as the mainstays of everyday life. It would be incorrect, however, to view the Boggs Center and the Concerned Citizens of Northwest Goldberg as the only groups working on the revitalization of the commons shared by African American and other ethnic groups in Detroit. The Foundation for Agricultural Renewal in Michigan (F.A.R.M.) runs an organic farm that supports youth programs and other community activities. There is also a group called Detroit Co-Housing that is developing an environmentally informed approach to co-housing in North Corktown for mixed-income families. The Sierra Club of Detroit focuses much of its attention on environmental-justice issues, working closely with members of CPR, the Boggs Center, Lead Busters, and other groups.

Perhaps the most nationally visible group working to reverse the blight and negative energy that is often found in areas of extreme urban poverty is Motor City Blight Busters, which is headed by John J. George. George's life took a new direction when he woke up one morning to find that the house next door had been turned into a meeting place for crack and other drug users. His immediate response was to secure the house by boarding up the windows and doors. From there, he brought together other members of the community concerned with replacing burned out and abandoned houses and buildings with new affordable houses—and with restoring buildings that could be used by community artists and musicians. Murals depicting important African-American leaders, as well as the vision of the local community for what their commons can become, are now replacing the fading advertisements for cigarettes and beer on the sides of buildings. The Motor City Blight Busters also sponsors Public Art Workz, which is headed by Charles "Chazz" Miller and Aurora Harris. Their respective energies and talents (Chazz being the visual artist and Aurora being the writer and poet) have helped to create the physical space for local artists, musicians, writers, and master woodworkers to work and to put on community performances. They also are models for the youth of the community of how the arts can serve to strengthen self-respect and mutual support within the community. In effect, the many activities supported by the Blight Busters organization represent what can be achieved when the values of working for the common good and respecting the creative energies and self-reliance within the community replace the competitive and consumer-oriented individualism that impoverishes the commons.

The Catherine Ferguson High School represents yet another way in which the commons is being renewed. The school is for young mothers and pregnant teens. It combines classes that lead to a high school diploma with hands-on agricultural experiences. The girls tend animals—ducks, chickens, rabbits, goats, three horses, and a cow—plant and tend vegetable gardens and a fruit orchard, bale hay in vacant lots, and even raised a barn in order to store the hay. They learn home-repairs skills from Jim Embry, who volunteers his time to teach them how to safely use power tools and hone skills they will later need to take care of everyday repairs. With the help of Detroit Summer volunteers from the Boggs Center they have tested soil in a mile square area around their school, learning to detect toxicity levels and to educate neighbors about the dangers of planting in contaminated soil. In addition to acquiring the education that will enable them to pursue higher education and employment, the young women are learning how to nurture their own children and neighbors, as well as plants and animals. This school represents yet another example of the effort to build self-reliance and to connect youth with the intergenerational knowledge of the community.

LARGER SIGNIFICANCE OF REVITALIZING
THE COMMONS

The efforts to revitalize the commons in Detroit's east side, Northwest Goldberg, and Old Redford neighborhoods have implications that go beyond creating toxic-free environments for African-American children to play in, providing fresh vegetables for the community's elderly, and raising community awareness of how to alleviate the immediate impact of poverty. The degree of poverty in Detroit, which is not limited to the African-American community, can be seen in the fact that some 30,000 residents had their water and electricity turned off during the winter of 2003. This led to the social services agency taking the children from the unheated homes and placing them in foster care and in juvenile detention facilities. As learned from past experience, challenging the city policies that lead to this kind of suffering and mistreatment cannot be done by individuals, but only by the collective voice of the community. The creation of this collective voice is only one of the goals of a revitalized commons. Unlike city council politics where developers and outsiders who have an economic interest exert an influence over decisions that affect the lives of the already marginalized ethnic groups, the collective voice of the commons represents the expression of grassroots democracy.

There are other implications of revitalizing the commons that also need to be recognized. One of the challenges facing other marginalized groups such as the Latino/Chicano, Asian American, indigenous Americans, and Hawaiian Americans, among others, is how to retain the genuine cultural achievements and practices that have been made by previous generations—achievements and practices that are essential to a positive self-identity and to empowerment as more self-reliant communities. The many expressions of enclosure that accompany the continuing spread of industrial culture involve more than a transaction that leads to a deed of ownership, the patenting of a gene line and a people's knowledge of biodiversity, and the commodification of a cultural group's expressive culture. The dynamics of enclosure also become part of a person's consciousness and self-identity. The taken-for-granted acceptance of the many forms that enclosure now takes (e.g., privatization of water, the airwaves, entertainment, health care, craft knowledge, and so forth) now alters the subjective experiences of memory and the ability to imagine alternatives to what fits an industrial mode of existence. Few individuals, especially among the younger generation, are able to imagine alternatives to the continued deskilling of work. Fatalism too often is replacing memory with the result that there is little resistance to the further automation of work—even by those who are most directly affected.

The psychological impact of a culture that equates enclosure with progress is the widespread adoption of a taken-for-granted attitude toward aligning one's life-goals with those of the industrial culture. This is expressed in the relentless drive to acquire more and more material things—from property and consumer goods to the more symbolic expressions of culture. The pervasive influence of the cultural dynamics of enclosure can also be seen in the metaphorical nature of the language that influences our perceptions of everyday reality—even as it influences what will be ignored and thus unnamed. The latter is especially important as what is unnamed remains outside the realm of political discourse. The dominance in the use of the personal pronoun by speakers of English, as well as the mechanistic metaphors that are the basis of thinking about everything from agriculture to the human body, reinforce the industrial mindset—including the idea of the autonomous individual and the organic world as a series of problems that require re-engineering.

The spread of industrial culture has left few aspects of everyday life in the West that have not been turned into commodities and thus mediated by the values of the market. Clothes, preferences in music and other forms of expressive culture, food, relationships with nature, health care, toys, education, and now, with the widespread use of computers, even thought and communication, involve consumerism. In addition to the environmental damage that results from hyper-consumerism and the mounting indebtedness, it also involves living a life that is designed by the people who create the product, taste in fashion, entertainment, focus of conversation, and criteria for judging the character and success of others.

It is in the dynamics of this increasing dependence upon consumerism and the experts who create the next cultural fad and technological innovation that the problem of identity that many marginalized cultural groups are coping with must be understood. And it is in the revitalization of the commons, which represents the most direct form of resistance to the spread of industrial culture, that many of these groups may find their own historically rooted approaches to resistance.

The revitalization of the commons—regardless of whether it is in rural Kansas, the mesas of the Hopi Nation, the neighborhoods of Detroit, or an upscale middle-class neighborhood—represents the ecologically intelligent and culturally affirming way to heal the cultural self-alienation that is caused by the industrial culture's emphasis on consumerism. Indeed, the many ways in which the culture of consumerism requires adopting its values and ways of thinking—competitive and acquisitive individualism, equating success and happiness with owning the high-status symbols of the marketplace, receptivity to being influenced by the media, rejection of intergenerational knowledge and traditions, and indifference to the ecological and social consequences of a hyper-consumer lifestyle—is at the center of what can be called the politics of identity that is being debated within different marginalized cultural groups. This debate is even taking place on the fringes of the middle class.

OVERLOOKING THE COMMONS: THE CRITIQUE OF ASSIMILATION IN THE DISCOURSE ON RACE

As Euro Americans, we are not qualified to enter into a discussion of the politics of identity of other cultural groups. We are especially unqualified to suggest how to resolve the arguments presented by leading African-American intellectuals such as Cornel West, Henry Louis Gates, Manning Marable, and bell hooks, and by educational theorists concerned with social justice issues about whether the African-American middle class is engaging in an assimilation strategy that creates the illusion that racism is no longer the dominant characteristic of American society. Nor do we want to insert ourselves into West's and Marable's reflections on why the African-American intellectual has only marginalized relevance to the African-American underclass. What we wish to do, and have a right to do, is to juxtapose the silences in the writings of West, hooks, Gates, Marable, and the educational theorists with the efforts to revitalize the commons in the east side and northwest neighborhoods of Detroit. We also wish to consider whether the ideas of the African-American intellectual leaders and the educational theorists support both the immediate and long-term goals of creating the postindustrial society that is being called Adamah.

West, Gates, Marable, hooks, and educational theorists such as Stephen Nathan Haymes and Henry Giroux have a clear understanding of how the dynamics of commodification fosters a form of individualism that views involvement in the networks of community as constraints on getting ahead. For these writers the failure of the African-American middle class is, in part, a result of seeking equal participation in the Euro-American middle class consumer-oriented culture. This assimilation strategy, as Haymes puts it, creates the illusion of a "color blind" consciousness, which he argues was also the goal of the civil rights movement. This state of consciousness, according to both Haymes and West, marginalizes the cultural differences between Euro and African Americans by representing the level of education as the determining factor. An extension of this way of thinking is to view the African Americans who receive the same level of education and the same economic opportunities as no different from the members of the Euro-American middle class. Marable and Gates develop similar critiques. The criticism of these writers is that in gaining access to the Euro-American middle class the African Americans adopt the mentality of the colonizing culture. For West and Haymes, this process of assimilation contributes to the loss of leadership in the formation of alternative African-American identities that challenge the assumptions and practices of racism.

This is the part of the debate that we are not qualified to pass judgment on other than to point out that the arguments against assimilation are based on double-bind thinking where education and economic success are experienced and analyzed as a betrayal of the larger segment of the African-American community that is still mired in poverty and limited opportunities. The other hard edge of the double bind is that the African Americans who resist assimilation to the values and patterns of thinking of the Euro-American middle class then share in the economic poverty of the African-American underclass. West identifies the double bind more in terms of the betrayal of one's self-identity and history as an African American. As he puts it,

These courageous yet limited black efforts to combat racist cultural practices uncritically accepted non-black conventions and standards in two ways. First, they proceeded in an *assimilationist manner* that set out to show that black people were really like white people—thereby eliding differences (in history, culture) between whites and blacks. Black specificity and particularity was thus banished in order to gain white acceptance and approval. Second, these black responses rested upon a homogenizing impulse that assumed that all black people were really alike—hence obliterating differences (class, gender, region, sexual orientation) between black peoples. I submit that there are elements of truth in both claims, yet the conclusions are unwarranted owing to the basic fact that non-black paradigms set the terms of the replies. (1993a: 17)

Arguing against this "homogenizing impulse," West goes on to note that African-American identities vary widely in terms of differences in gender, class, region, and nations.

In a similar vein, writers Henry Louis Gates and Manning Marable have also argued that assimilationism has had an adverse impact upon identity formation within the African-American community. In an autobiographical response to W. E. B. DuBois's well-known essay "The Talented Tenth," Gates writes of a growing disenchantment of the black middle class as he grew to adulthood, describing the psychological effects as "dashed hopes: of great expectations, and the mourning after" for those who believed that "making it" was the answer to the suffering among African-American communities (21). Describing a growing gap between affluence and poverty in the African-American community as contributing to both "political retrenchment and the very real phenomenon of survivor's guilt," he comments,

> On a rational level, of course, we know that black prosperity doesn't derive from black poverty; on a symbolic level, however, the chronic hardship of a third of black America is a standing reproach to those of us who once dreamed of collective uplift. (1996: 25)

In his recent book *The Great Wells of Democracy* (2002), Manning Marable also contributes to this analysis of African-American identity, and like West he locates the foundations of assimilationism in a neoliberal tradition that fundamentally changed African Americans both culturally and psychologically. In an historical analysis of desegregation, he likens the process and its effects on the African-American community to the profound changes imposed on traditional African societies by European colonization. Describing his own childhood where Jim Crow laws meant living "in a world apart," he argues that segregation meant that African-American community members—doctors, lawyers, teachers, barbers, ministers, and builders—were forced to depend upon each other, and thus developed important cultural and psychological bonds quite distinct from Euro-American culture. Desegregation had a fragmenting effect on these bonds, even as it offered some people economic and social opportunities.

> But from the perspective of liberal integrationism, black people generally believed that the total desegregation of white institutions was identical with the pursuit of racial progress and individual upward mobility. We were, in

effect, obligated by the weight of our own history to boldly go where no Negroes had gone before. . . . The weakness of the black community's cultural and public intellectual infrastructure, as well as the prestige and material benefits to be derived by assimilation into or cooperation with white established institutions, has produced a growing elite of black "intercessors" or go-between facilitators along society's color line. (2002: 170–171)

For Marable, as for other African-American intellectuals, the push to prove themselves capable and even powerful within white institutions has the paradoxical effect of distancing them from the communities they intended to "lift up." The consequences are severe both in terms of the paradox of identity formation among the middle class, as well as the real separation between middle-class intellectuals and the people who they intend to serve. As we will discuss below, this critique of assimilationism has led Marable to turn his attention to the grassroots work of activists in city neighborhoods where the demands of everyday life create ad hoc formations of locally inspired groups.

There are two issues that are not raised in the debates over assimilation and the loss of African-American identities. The first has to do with the ecological implications of participating in the hyper-consumer oriented middle class. The other issue pertains to an equally important phenomenon: namely, how the reliance upon Western technologies, even by African Americans living in extreme poverty and within ghettoized communities, leads to a degree of cultural assimilation that West and the educational theorists do not recognize.

In considering the connections between assimilation to the hyper-consumer culture and the rapid changes we are now witnessing in the Earth's natural systems, it is important to keep in mind the point made by Peter McLaren: namely, that social reforms need to create "equal access to the material necessities of human survival" (2000: 262). It is also important to keep in mind that questioning the environmentally disruptive culture that some African Americans, as well as members of other minority groups, are assimilating into also requires questioning the excessive consumption that the majority of Euro-Americans now take for granted. From an environmental perspective it does not really matter whether the SUV that puts extra tons of greenhouse gases into the atmosphere and requires the expansion of American imperialism in order to ensure a steady supply of cheap gasoline, is driven by a Euro or African American. Similarly, there is no difference in the environmental impact between African and Euro Americans when they shop at one of the megastores where the goods have been shipped in from different parts of the world, when they frequent the industrial fast-food outlets, and when they become followers of the latest consumer fad dictated by the media.

What needs to be in the forefront of any discussion of cultural identity, equity, and social justice are the changes that will lead to cultural practices that have a smaller ecological footprint. At the same time, the need for providing the material necessities of life must also be considered. Reforms in the dominant middle-class culture must also take into account the need to ensure that future generations will also have the material necessities as well as opportunities for socially and individually meaningful work. Unfortunately, these issues are not part of the current discussion of whether assimilation is a continuation of Euro-American racism—disguised as liberal social reforms.

How the changes in natural systems will affect the African-American underclass is also ignored in West's frequent references to the failure of African-American intellectuals to be taken seriously within the larger African-American community. As a philosopher who ignores environmental issues, such as environmental racism and the way in which corporations circumvent environmental regulations by moving their production facilities overseas (thus adding to the loss of jobs for African Americans), it should not be a great surprise that West and other African-American intellectuals find their audience mostly in university settings—which along with the media are the primary institutions of cultural assimilation.

TECHNOLOGY AND ASSIMILATION

The other issue that is ignored in the heated debates over the politics of identity, including the viewing of assimilation as a betrayal of the African-American experience in America, is related to the view of technology that is still dominant in Euro-American culture. That is, the view that holds that technology is, at the same time, both the expression of progress and culturally neutral. West and hooks, along with the social justice educational theorists, are critical of how capitalism leads to the misuse of technology: specifically how it places profits above the potential socially constructive uses of technology. But what they overlook is the way in which the use of modern technologies contributes to the assimilation to a Western form of individual subjectivity. For example, working on an assembly line, using a computer, relying upon print as the basis of encoding and decoding messages, using a car, and taking one of many drugs, and so forth, are not culturally neutral experiences. Each of these technologies, and many more that could be cited, incorporate the patterns of thinking and values of the people who designed them. This can be seen in how the cell phone selects certain aspects of human communication for amplification, while preventing other aspects from being communicated. Voice and, now, pictures, are communicated, but the non-verbal cues that are so important to understanding relationships are omitted. What a technology amplifies and marginalizes is part of a colonizing (assimilation) process when it is used by a non-Western person. The assembly line amplifies repetitive motions and a sense of indifference toward the social usefulness of what is being produced. Putting in the time and earning a wage displaces the importance of exercising one's own craft skills and knowledge and producing something useful that can be exchanged with others in the community. It also eliminates the possibility of controlling the pace of work and of subordinating work to the ebb and flow of reciprocal community relationships. Working at a fast-food outlet, which is organized as an assembly line that encodes the assumptions and values of the people who created it, is just another example of cultural assimilation. Youth, regardless of cultural background, are being assimilated to the experience of working for a wage—regardless of how mind-numbing and repetitive it is. And this experience is not likely to lead them to think of work as a reciprocal obligation within the community (that is, returned without the expectation of being paid a wage) as is the case within many non-Western cultures.

Similarly, cultural messages encoded in print, which are now combined with powerful visual images of success and a higher social standing, involve an even more complex process of cultural amplification and reduction. The combined print and visual messages connect the viewer with the patterns of thought and values of the corporate centers of power, thus marginalizing the importance of intergenerational knowledge and values that are renewed through face-to-face communication. Unlike face-to-face communication, especially when it involves the sharing of intergenerational experience, the various media technologies do not allow for a sense of mutuality or accountability. Print and television, for example, are based on a sender/receiver model of communication and involve asymmetrical power relationships. That is, they involve the acceptance of a hierarchical and consciousness-transforming form of communication. If the readers or viewers have the requisite background knowledge, personal memory, critical thought, and the valuing of the interests of the commons, they may come into play in how the messages are interpreted. But if they lack the background knowledge, the assimilation may be unmediated by the individual's critical and knowledgeable judgment.

The assimilation power of print and visual images can be seen in how youth from many different cultural backgrounds become alienated from the traditions of their communities. To relate the process of assimilation directly to the critics of African-American assimilation, we can see that they present ideas in the rational, decontextualized, non-reciprocal patterns that are required by a print-based form of consciousness. They are prime examples of the point we are making about how the use of Western technologies leads to cultural assimilation, even when the technology is being used to argue for alternative cultural identities. Just to cite one example, the length of the sentences found in the writings of West and hooks is quite different from the length of sentences that would be part of face-to-face discourse. Context, personal memory, and accountability in terms of the cultural norms governing discourse would also be profoundly different from the print-mediated form of their discourse.

Perhaps the most powerful example of how a technology mediates subjective experience in ways that assimilate (colonize) consciousness to the cultural patterns that are amplified by the technology can be seen in the use of computers. While West, Marable, Gates, Haymes, and the other theorists who are addressing the issue of African-American assimilation might argue that computers are beyond the reach of the African-American underclass, there are others who advocate that making computers accessible is the route out of poverty, and into the middle-class consumer culture. This argument is problematic in many ways. The point we want to make is more directly related to the question of whether the use of Western technologies is not in itself a process of assimilation to the dominant Western industrial culture.

As pointed out in *Let Them Eat Data* (2000), the cultural amplification and reduction characteristics of computers are determined by what can and cannot be digitized—and in being digitized is fundamentally transformed, such as the transformation of the spoken narrative into a printed text. In asking what cannot be digitized without being reduced to an abstract text or visual image, we find that tacit cultural knowledge and patterns, context, embodied experiences, personal memory, culturally specific patterns of reciprocity, spoken narratives, ceremonies, languaging processes that reproduce the culture's moral codes that govern human/nature relationships, and mythopoetic narratives that are the basis of the culture's way of knowing and value system are high on the list. What computers select for amplification are the cultural patterns that are valued in an industrially based culture: abstract and culturally context-free information and data, a conduit view of language, a sense of temporality that reinforces the idea that the individual decides whether the past or future has any relevance, print and visual images that reinforce the Cartesian myth of the individual as an autonomous thinker. While we do not want to be interpreted as suggesting that computers are not useful, we do want to emphasize that the forms of knowledge and relationships that cannot be digitized without being fundamentally transformed are the basis of communities that understand the importance of the commons.

The argument will be made by environmentally oriented scientists that computers are vital to understanding how natural systems are being degraded, and we agree with this point. But the more important point still stands: namely, that computers amplify (reinforce) the individually centered form of consciousness (being an autonomous thinker, a subjective sense of temporality, and being a participant in a sender/receiver process of communication that marginalizes the culturally reproductive characteristics of language) that is required by the industrial culture that is a major contributor to the ecological crisis that scientists now warn us about.

The issue that is being ignored by African-American intellectuals and social theorists is that assimilation to the culture of the Euro Americans who created the technology is an inescapable accompaniment of using the computer. An example of this lack of attention on the part of these intellectuals can be found in Manning Marable's uncritical description of demands by participants in an African American Grassroots Leadership conference held in Cincinnati in the spring of 2001 that, among other suggestions, called for "the Internet and digital knowledge" as "keys toward the future development of the black ghetto" (2002: 201). This process of assimilation even occurs when the computer is used for emancipatory goals. We witnessed similar contradictory effects in the efforts of the Zapatistas to gain support for their struggle to free themselves from the colonizing control of the Mexican government through the use of the Internet.

It would not be incorrect to claim that the role computers now play in undermining the diversity of the world's languages by privileging a small handful of the widely spoken and written languages is a technologically enforced form of assimilation that is irreversible. It also needs to be kept in mind that the use of computers in preserving the near-extinct languages is not the same as revitalizing them to their former complexity and vitality.

VISIONS OF RESISTANCE AND EMANCIPATION THAT NEGLECT THE COMMONS

The constant reference to race in the writings of West and hooks, as well as the educational theorists, rather than to specific differences in cultural practices and ways of thinking, makes it difficult to discern which culture practices are shared by social classes, and by different segments of the African and Euro-American communities. West, hooks, and Marable are very clear about the destructive nature of capitalism, including how the emphasis on the promotion of consumerism now reaches down to African Americans who live below the poverty line. However, the closest they get to describing specific cultural differences is in their references to how the African-American middle class has adopted the values and thought patterns of liberalism, where the emphasis is on individualism, the pursuit of self-interest, and on the drive to expand the opportunities within the Euro-American middle class—which West and hooks view as the main objective of the civil rights movement.

One has to read carefully to obtain an understanding of the culture of African Americans that continues to be marginalized by racial prejudice, their history of being economically exploited, and the still largely hidden record of their cultural achievements. West cites what he refers to as the two "organic" intellectual traditions in African-American life: "the black Christian tradition of preaching and the black musical tradition of performance" (1999: 306). Beyond these two examples, which are framed as past traditions, the issue of future cultural developments remains problematic.

First, there is the question of whether the elimination of racism alone would lead to the oppressed African Americans creating new or renewing past forms of cultural expression that differ substantially from the industrial consumer-oriented culture of the African and Euro-American middle class. This question is particularly relevant to whether the efforts of the Northwest Goldberg community and the Boggs Center represent an alternative culture that would be supported by the African-American underclass.

The second question relates to whether the strategy of achieving emancipation from the constraints of racism would lead to an alternative post industrial culture as envisioned for the east side and Northwest Goldberg neighborhoods of Detroit. Or, would the deep patterns of thinking that underlie the industrial culture undermining what remains of the networks of community self-sufficiency and the self-renewing capacity of natural systems simply remain or be reinforced? We shall return to this question when we consider how the African-American intellectuals, as well as the educational theorists who write about the elimination of racism, embrace the ideas of Paulo Freire.

The characteristics of a culture that represents an alternative to what West, hooks, and Haymes variously describe as the consumer crazed, racist patterns of the Euro-American middle class are never explicitly described. These characteristics begin to emerge, however, when special attention is given to what these authors affirm—which is treated as marginal to their discussions of the degrading impact of past and current expressions of racism. In the chapter "Class and the Politics of Living Simply," hooks suggests an alternative path of cultural development for African Americans that is a core feature of the postindustrial society envisioned for the east side and Northwest Goldberg neighborhoods of Detroit. "To see the poor as ourselves we must want for the poor what we want for ourselves. By living simply," she continues, "we express our solidarity with the poor and our recognition that the gluttonous consumption must end." Thus, the values of caring, compassion, and sharing are to be the basis for redefining wealth: the wealth of relationships and reciprocity rather than in material terms. As she put it, "solidarity with the poor is the only path that can lead our nation back to a vision of community that can effectively challenge and eliminate violence and exploitation" (2000: 48–49). It is important here to not interpret hooks as claiming that poverty builds character. Rather she is highlighting the values and practices of community she witnessed during her youth when the pursuit of material wealth was not made the central goal of life.

West's understanding of the strengths of African-American communities can be gleaned from his description of the damaging effects of the spread of drugs. In lamenting the impact of drugs, West turns to a description of African-American civil society—as it was and as it should become again. These civil communities, according to West, included "the family, church, fraternity, sorority, beauty shop, barber shop, shopkeeper, funeral parlor that used to be in place and served as the infrastructures that transmitted the values and sensibilities to notions of self-respect and self-esteem (that) still had some possibility of distribution across the black community" (1993b: 149). Of particular concern to West is how the "loss of ties at birth of ascending and descending generations, a loss of ties to both predecessor and progeny" has undermined the creation of positive self-identities within the larger social context of negative images. What West is affirming is the importance of face-to-face communities that allow people to negotiate meanings, learn the codes of moral reciprocity within a variety of social contexts, and to find one's identity within the frameworks of the intergenerational narratives that connect the community of memory to a specific place.

While West dreams of a return to civil society within the African-American community, and hooks remembers a better time when close mutually beneficial relationships characterized life in African-American communities, Manning Marable looks to current practices within city neighborhoods as a source of hope and political power. Studying grassroots political movements in cities across the nation, Marable argues that coalitions of non-profit community-based organizations and other groups have the power to reshape the meaning of community and rejuvenate political efficacy for African Americans (2000, 2002). This work seems promising on the surface for the way it begins to connect to the kinds of neighborhood work we have seen in Detroit.

For example, responding to concerns about a fatal disconnect between African-American intellectuals and people's lives within communities, he argues that "scholars should first listen and learn from the people themselves" (2000, xiii). Reasserting arguments about the limits of assimilationism and commenting upon on-the-ground democratic work in cities across the nation, he writes:

> In order to challenge the effects of neoliberalism and revive those suffering from civil death, a black political project must be grounded in grassroots struggles around practical questions of daily life. Such struggles bring into the public arena diverse and sometimes contradictory ideological and social forces. . . . It is at the grassroots level that blacks might begin the difficult task of constructing new social theory and political strategies, extrapolating from their collective experiences and practices of neighborhood and community based activism. This approach to politics starts with the micro-battles of neighborhood empowerment to bring about change in the macro-contexts of national and international processes impacting African Americans. (2002: 205)

Later in the chapter he writes that in learning from community-based coalitions, African-American activists should not presume "to impose a set of theoretical perspectives upon these local formations as they emerge," but rather to put together "new strategies and theory" based on these developing struggles. He also makes clear that such learning must take into account work being done by working poor in multiethnic, multiracial communities and recognize "the powerful roles black women activists play as the central organizers of many of these community based groups."

> We need new organizational forms to accomplish our goals: not a party based on a vanguard, cadre-type organization, which unfortunately characterized much of the left in the 1960s and 1970s, but a national network of black radical activists who are directly involved in community organizing, feminist, labor, lesbian, gay, and progressive black nationalist causes. (pp. 214–215)

While Marable's focus upon local, on-the-ground activism is notable, and his argument for networks among these groups is important, he unfortunately misses an important dimension of the micro-level work in the neighborhoods. That is, in his emphasis on "the battle" and on solutions that require "new strategies and theories," he relies too heavily on a model of radical change (in his vision coming from the neighborhoods rather than imposed from above), and overlooks forms of resistance being created from place-bound relationships and intergenerational traditions of mutual aid, care, and respect being revived among people in cities such as Detroit. As we will detail below, along with West, hooks, and others, his faith in an emancipatory politics betrays a liberal ideology that represents change as inherently progressive. In spite of Marable's focus on grassroots activism, his writings contain an implicit paternalistic view of those he writes about. His emphasis on *creating new social theory* and even the title of the chapter detailing this analysis—"Building Democracy from Below: Community Empowerment"—suggests that Marable, like the other prominent African-American educational intellectuals, paradoxically locates himself as above those in the neighborhoods, even while he critiques this "vanguard" position. Because his focus is still primarily on the work of activists as change agents, Marable substitutes an elitist notion of empowerment for a true recognition of and respect for local relationships and cultural wisdom. And because he does not begin from an understanding of the commons, his analysis stops short of actually recognizing "the practical questions of daily life" in the richness of place-bound relationships and practices, and overlooks the powerful forms of resistance being engaged as people take care of themselves, the land, and each other.

Stephen Haymes, the educational theorist, reiterates the importance of place, or what he refers to as "urban space," both to the positive formation of self-identities and as sites of resistance to the colonizing characteristics of Euro-America's industrial culture. To paraphrase Haymes, African-American public spaces are not simply "spaces of opposition." They are, more importantly, "spaces of self-actualization" (1995:138). However, Haymes stops short of explaining the forms of cultural expression that will emerge from the process of self-actualization, which is a phrase that is still prominent in Euro-American pop psychology.

Taken together, these fragmentary descriptions of what African Americans should want in their communities, and what will differentiate their culture from that of the dominant middle class, are not too different from the characteristics of other ethnic communities before the homogenizing impact of the media and the growing emphasis on consumerism. West's description of an intergenerationally connected community is also similar to the communities of rural America before the industrialization of agriculture led to the decline of rural communities. What is distinctive about West's vision of an African-American civil community is that, in terms of scale, it is smaller—with control centered in the private ownership of small businesses and services. The megastores that now drain the economic life from the physical center of communities, and reinforce the use of cars, introduce another change that does not fit with a basic characteristic of an intergenerationally connected community. That is, they change the pattern of face-to-face interactions that are essential to the vitality of democracy. The interactions in the megastores and shopping malls are less frequently those of neighbors who renew relationships through their greetings and incidental conversations, and the interactions between strangers also lack the sensitivity to differences in outlook and values that characterize the more face-to-face communities. Rather, the interactions are generally within the context of the customer/clerk relationship, and the passing of strangers. Like the computer which is supposed to network people together, the mega-stores and shopping malls give the appearance of vast numbers of people interacting together, but the reality is that both the computer and the shopping malls isolate people from each other.

The small, face-to-face community that West suggests as representative of one of the strengths of former African-American communities also has another virtue not found in the megastores and industrial food and consumer goods outlets. That is, the small privately owned business provides a different kind of work experience than is found in the corporate-controlled business. One of the differences is in the accountability that is present for both employer and employee when they know each other as neighbors, and as members of families that have interacted over generations. While West's description of the African-American civil community may appear as both highly romanticized and as a case of nostalgia for a return to simpler times, the revitalization efforts of the communities of Detroit, are in fact, very much in line with the values of West and hooks.

But there are two major differences that separate the thinking of the African-American intellectuals from that of the Northwest Goldberg community, the Boggs Center, and the Committee for the Political Resurrection of Detroit. The first is that the postindustrial society that the latter groups are working for is to be multiethnic and thus multicultural. One of the projects of the Boggs Center is the rebuilding of what was the center of the Chinese-American community that was located in the lower Cass Corridor neighborhood. The writings of West, hooks, Marable, and Haymes emphasize two distinct categories: the oppressor culture of Euro America and the oppressed African Americans—with the African-American intellectuals being oppressed by both the Euro-American culture and by the indifference shown them by the African-American underclass. The thinking behind the revitalization of the Detroit commons is explicit about the importance of the cultural contributions of different ethnic cultures.

There is another even more significant difference between the thinking of West, hooks, Marable, and the educational theorists who are addressing the problem of racism, and the approach being taken to revitalize the commons in Detroit. The leaders of the Northwest Goldberg community and the Boggs Center incorporate the ancient idea of the commons into their renewal projects. This includes the different physical aspects of the commons (what is shared by everyone—or should be) such as water, soil, plants, animals, and the air people breathe. Restoring these environmental aspects of the commons that have been badly degraded by Detroit's industrial history is thus one of their central concerns. Members of these communities clear vacant lots of old rusty industrial machines in order to plant community gardens, and monitor the level of toxins in the soil (especially the presence of lead) to ensure that children's playgrounds are as safe as possible. Their concern with protecting what remains of the commons can be seen in their efforts to resist the privatization of Detroit's municipal water systems, and to have the industrial plants that release toxic chemicals into the atmosphere shut down. That their efforts are only partially successful can be attributed, in part, to the racism that still enters into political and corporate decision making, and to their lack of economic resources.

The long-term goal, as envisioned in the Adamah project, is to restore the ecosystems—streams, fields, plants, and animal life—in ways that will enable the communities of the Detroit east side to become self-sufficient in terms of meeting their need for water. The replacement of the industrial approach to production with decentralized community-centered producers of goods and services that facilitate an economy of exchange and barter is viewed as changing the quality of air that the people rely upon. This awareness that the revitalization of the symbolic and economic aspects of the commons is dependent upon a radical revitalization of the natural systems is what is missing in the writing of West, hooks, and the educational theorists concerned about overcoming racism.

For the most part, these theorists ignore both the nature and extent of environmental racism, and the steps needed to restore the natural environment. This is especially surprising, particularly since environmental racism has been the central focus of many African-American neighborhoods. As far back as 1991, a coalition of African Americans, Native Americans, Latinos, and Asian Americans held the First Nation of People of Color Environmental Leadership Summit in Washington, D.C.—and has continued to meet on a yearly basis. A second notable exception to the lack of attention to environmental issues in the writings of West and hooks appears in a statement called the Principles of Unity, written as an organizing mission for the Black Radical Congress—a meeting held in 1998 of more than two thousand progressive African-American activists and intellectuals, and which was described in Manning Marable and Leith Mullings's book, *Let Nobody Turn Us Around: Voices of Resistance, Reform, and Renewal* (2000). Listed among a whole host of commitments including the equal treatment of women, lesbian, gay, bisexual, and transgendered people, the struggle against police brutality, fair labor practices, the protection of public education, and so on, item VII in the document (also referred to as the "freedom agenda") reads

We will struggle for a clean and healthy environment.
    We will fight for a society in which the welfare of people and the natural environment takes precedence over commercial profits and political expedi-

ency. We will work to protect, preserve and enhance society's and the planet's natural heritage—forests lakes rivers oceans, mountain ranges, animal life, flora and fauna. In the US we will struggle against environmental racism by fighting for laws that strictly regulate the disposal of hazardous industrial wastes and that forbid both the discriminatory targeting of poor and non-white communities for dumping and despoilment of the natural environment. (Marable 2000: 630)

According to Marable and Mullings, the BRC was organized to establish a network of local organizing committees to support "political activities including anti-police brutality cases, economic justice campaigns and the struggle to defend public education" (625) among African-American people across the nation. In fact, in response to this call for local action, the BRC met in Detroit in 2000, attended by some of the members of CPR, including Charles Simmons, but apparently has lost steam as either a local or national force. And while the environmental justice concerns may have had significance for people like Simmons and others in Detroit, they were clearly not central to this prominent group of intellectuals such as West and hooks—which may be one of the reasons they are not taken seriously by grassroots activists.

LIMITATIONS OF THE FREIREAN LEGACY
FOR REVITALIZING THE COMMONS

There is another characteristic of the writings of West, hooks, and many of the educational theorists writing on the problem of racism that is both problematic and a source of irony. Both West and hooks acknowledge the importance of the ideas of Paulo Freire to the development of their own thinking. In *Teaching to Transgress: Education as the Practice of Freedom* (1994), hooks recounts how the ideas of Freire influenced her approach to teaching when she was on the faculty of Oberlin College. West goes further by claiming that the publication of *Pedagogy of the Oppressed* "was a world-historical event for counter-hegemonic theorists and activists in search of new ways to link social theory to narratives of human freedom" (1993a: 179). Educational theorists such as Henry Giroux and Peter McLaren, among others, continue to make Freire's ideas the basis of their consciousness-transforming pedagogy. As publishers avoid publishing books that raise questions about the cultural assumptions that underlie Freire's ideas, he continues to attract new followers such as Haymes to his enlightenment way of thinking.

Unnoticed by West, hooks, and Freire's many followers among educational theorists is that a pedagogy based on critical reflection, and represented as the one and only true approach to knowledge, is *not* "counter-hegemonic" as West claimed. If attention is given to the deep, taken-for-granted cultural assumptions that Freire's pedagogy is based upon it becomes readily apparent that these are the same assumptions that were the basis of the Industrial Revolution—and continue to be the basis of the digital phase of the Industrial Revolution we have now entered. Critical reflection, which Freire claims should be the basis of each generation renaming the world (with the expectation that the next generation will emancipate itself from the naming of the previous generation) (1974 edition, p. 76), is also the basis of Western science, to the problem-solving that leads to new technologies—and to the overturning of the technologies created by the previous generation. To propose as Freire does that critical reflection, this hallmark of the Western scientific/technological form of consciousness, should be the basis of achieving the highest expression of human potential, and that it should displace all the other ways in which the different cultures of the world encode, renew, and transform their various forms of knowledge cannot be interpreted in any other way than as the expression of a colonizing mentality.

The God-words of the liberal lexicon such as "emancipation," "freedom," and "dialogue" cannot hide that promoting the idea that there is only one approach to knowledge supports the forces of globalization. Critical reflection is vital in certain contexts, but it has a long history that goes back at least to Socrates—and the history of its use by philosophers and other theorists has not always led to improving the lives of the people who were to be uplifted by its emancipatory powers. To make the point more directly, West, hooks, and the educational theorists in the Freirean tradition of thinking have ignored the history of how different groups have used critical reflection to achieve their own ends—including the development of new technologies that would eliminate the need for workers. Also, they have ignored how to reconcile the idea that critical reflection is the only valid approach to knowledge with the value of cultural self-determination in a world where there are still thousands of knowledge systems.

The non-hegemonic way of thinking about the use of critical inquiry would be to understand that its emancipatory potential always depends upon the cultural context, and that its use needs to be balanced by giving attention to what needs to be conserved. And what needs to be conserved requires giving attention to what contributes to the well-being of the commons—which includes, as pointed our earlier, both the natural environment and the symbolic and social practices of the human community.

Whether the ideas of Freire provide the best approach to overcoming racism, to revitalizing the commons, and to resisting the industrial forces of globalization is not only relevant to any consideration of the strengths and weaknesses of the ideas of West and hooks, but also to educational approaches being taken to renew the commons of Detroit's east side. Critical reflection, and even John Dewey's approach to experimental problem solving (which he also viewed as the only valid approach to knowledge) are important to understanding the nature of oppressive and outmoded traditions. The mistake made by Freire's followers is that they interpret critical reflection as originating with him. The much older idea of a liberal education has always been based on the importance of fostering critical reflection—but within the tradition of thinking established by Western philosophers and social theorists.

If we can recognize that critical reflection did not originate with Freire, we can perhaps ask about the other traditions of Western thinking that buttress his idea of achieving our highest potential as humans through an ongoing process of critical reflection. As pointed out elsewhere (Bowers, 1987, 1993, 1995, 2001), Freire's core idea, which he expressed as "to exist humanly, is to name the world, to change it" (1974: 76) is based on a number of other assumptions taken for granted in the West by the men and women who are transforming the process of colonization from a religious mission into a full-scale business enterprise. These deep cultural assumptions, which cause Freire's followers to embrace critical reflection with such unquestioning fervor, include the idea that change is the expression of a linear and irreversible form of progress. Indeed, one does not find in the writing of Freire and his followers any questioning of the possibilities that change may not always represent progress.

The other cultural assumptions that buttress Freire's core ideas about what is essential to being human, and the need to think critically, include the anthropocentric way of representing humans as being separate from the environment. One of the ironies ignored by Freire's followers is that in *Education for Critical Consciousness* (1973) he equates the non-critically reflective individual with being driven, like an animal, by biological necessity. He not only slanders the cultures in the "backward regions of

Brazil" but also the many expressions of intelligence of the non-human world—which many non-anthropocentric cultures have learned from. Freire's anthropocentrism, which his followers have also embraced, accounts for the silence in his writings, and in the writings of all but a few of his followers, about the ecological crisis.

Other Western assumptions include the idea that the rational process (that is, critical reflection) is not culturally influenced, the idea that the primary goal of the individual is to achieve greater freedom, the idea that all traditions are sources of oppression that must be made explicit and transformed in terms of the individual's or social group's immediate perspective, and that the values that are to serve as momentary guides in a world of constant change will emerge from the process of critical reflection.

The success of the community-based efforts to revitalize the commons of the east side and Northwest Goldberg neighborhoods of Detroit will certainly depend upon the use of critical reflection about the sources of economic power that benefits from environmentally racist practices, the deliberate withholding of public services, and the other ways in which the state of poverty is being maintained. But success will also depend upon not taking for granted the other cultural assumptions that are shared by Freire and his followers. The commons, as pointed out elsewhere, involve a network of interdependencies that connect humans and the natural environment, and these interdependencies are also intergenerationally connected. These two realities point to the need for a more complex understanding of the role of education in achieving the vision of a postindustrial society.

An important question is whether the invoking of Freire's name to justify critical reflection (when it could be justified on the grounds of common sense—informed by tradition) also involves accepting the cultural assumptions that support the other dimensions of his thinking. Our preference would be to not use his name, just as we do not invoke Marx's name because of all of the culturally specific assumptions he took for granted. Why not just engage in critical reflection without suggesting that it originated with Freire? And why not engage in dialogue without attributing it to the insights of Freire (an attribution that also ignores Martin Buber's more nuanced understanding of dialogue)?

The more complex approach to education that is consistent with the idea of revitalizing the commons needs to be able to address what needs to be conserved as well as what needs to be changed. This more balanced approach, which is less driven by the myth of linear progress, requires rethinking not only how we are using such words as "emancipation" but also such words as "conservative." Unfortunately, the writings of West continue the liberal tradition of dichotomous thinking where the word conservative is associated with what is backward, oppressive, unjust, and the defense of special privileges. While revitalizing the commons in Detroit requires asking what needs to be conserved that contributes to the self-sufficiency of the African-American community that is shared with other ethnic groups, West restates the formulaic thinking that has given the word a pariah standing in the political lexicon of supposedly thoughtful and social justice–oriented people.

In *Prophetic Thoughts in Postmodern Times* (1993b), West describes conservatism in America as the unwillingness "to give up its racism, its sexism, its homophobia" (152). He further reduces the explanatory power of conservatism to a "focus on two terrains: discrimination in the market place and judgments made in the minds of people" (1993a: 252). West goes on to claim that there are three "basic versions of the conservative view of African-American oppression: the *market* version, the *sociobiology's* version, and the *cultureless* version" (1993a: 252–253). The market version is attributed to Milton Friedman's economic theory, which is a modern-day extrapolation of classical liberal ideas—which West acknowledges. Few people who understand the history of philosophical conservative thinking from Burke to Clinton Rosier would agree with West's attempt to identify the scientism of sociobiology with any other tradition than liberalism.

Having identified various supposed expressions of conservatism as the basis of racism, West is unable to acknowledge his own deeply held conservative ideas. For example, his comments about what he refers to as the "*natal* alienation, the loss of ties at birth of ascending and descending generations, the loss of ties to both predecessor and progeny" (1993a: 149) is a restatement of the core ideas of Edmund Burke, the founder of the tradition of philosophical conservatism in the West. A more accurate way of describing the tradition of racism would have been to refer to it as reactionary, and as an expression of *traditionalism*—a word that is used to represent the mistaken idea that traditions are static and unchanging. And if he felt that this word would be misunderstood by his readers, he could have use the term "reactionary" to describe the political orientation of racist thinkers and activists.

Having demonized the word "conservatism," West is left only with the vocabulary of liberalism, which is also the vocabulary of the people

promoting the further expansion of industrial culture. The idea of emancipation, which is central to the thinking of West, hooks, Marable, and the educational theorists, and to such other social justice advocates as Rabbi
Michael Lerner, who advocates "emancipatory spirituality" as the basis of
community, is also the goal of those promoting the expansion of a consumer-
dependent society. That is, emancipation of individuals from the traditions
of self-sufficiency within their communities is essential to the expansion
of industrial culture. In a word, the corporate culture also needs the
autonomous individual: that is, individuals who assume that their empowerment lies in the process of constant change.

Given the accelerating rate of environmental degradation, and the phenomenon of global warming that can no longer be denied, we face two fundamental questions. Should we address the social justice issues by emphasizing
the need for emancipating individuals so that they assume that their own
individual experience is sufficient for guiding the process of critical inquiry
that will lead to constructing their own ideas and values? Will this be an
effective way to resist the industrial forces that are globalizing the consumer,
individually centered culture that is now destroying the self-renewing capacity of the natural systems that life as we know it depends upon?

Or should we now view the conserving of the multiple dimensions of the
interdependent life-renewing processes that constitute the commons as the
more effective form of resistance? As the commons vary in terms of bioregions and cultures, the question also needs to take account of conserving
linguistic/cultural diversity, as well as the intergenerational knowledge that
represents alternatives to consumer-dependent lives.

The ecological crisis, which is having a greater adverse impact on
people already mired in poverty, requires a different approach than is
being taken by social justice theorists such as West, hooks, Marable,
Haymes, and the other followers of Freire. The tradition of decontextualized theory that leads to using a highly politicized vocabulary needs to be
replaced by a more context-specific discussion of what needs to be
changed and what needs to be conserved as sources of community and
individual empowerment.

The ecological crisis—the changes in the carbon cycle, the decline in
available potable water, the loss of regenerating capacity of the world's
fisheries, the loss of species, the loss of topsoil now estimated on a worldwide basis as 33 percent, chemical changes in the world's oceans and air—
provide the moral and political reference point that should now be beyond

debate. Cultural practices that further degrade the environment, contribute to environmental racism, deprive other cultures of their ability to be as self-reliant as is possible in this increasingly globalized world, and place in jeopardy the prospects of future generations, should be the focus of critical inquiry and change.

Cultural practices that enable its members to possess the intergenerational knowledge that is the source of greater self-sufficiency and that has a smaller adverse ecological impact need to be conserved through intergenerational mentoring, dialogue, and critique. These criteria must be assessed in terms of specific cultural contexts and bioregions, which means that pronouncements about the need for universal approaches to emancipation and freedom may serve more the psychological needs of the Western theorists than contribute to reversing the ecological and cultural trends that must now be addressed.

The problematic nature of theory that encourages emancipation while ignoring the cultural and environmental context can be seen by juxtaposing the on-the-ground efforts to renew the commons on the east side and in the Northwest Goldberg neighborhood of Detroit with the abstract writings of West, hooks, Marable, and the educational theorists who are followers of Freire. Aside from West's brief description of what constitutes a healthy African-American civil community, hooks's equally brief discussion of the alternative to "gluttonous consumerism," and Marable's limited vision of grassroots activism, most of what they write, while accurately focusing on the traditions of racism, has little relevance for understanding the importance (indeed, the radical nature) of what is being attempted by the leaders and community members of Detroit. In the 15 or so books written by West, hooks, and the educational theorists that are sitting on our desks, we have found only a single reference to the ecological crisis; nor did we find any discussion of the local traditions that need to be strengthened as part of revitalizing the commons.

In effect, the assumptions they share with the industrial culture they are so quick to criticize are responsible for their collective silence on the most important issue that must now be addressed by all of the world's cultures: namely, how to revitalize the traditions of self-reliance that have a smaller ecological footprint, and how to achieve a postindustrial future that is not dependent upon the exploitation and marginalization of any group of people. Again, this task has to be addressed on a culture-by-culture basis, and the importance of cultural self-determination (as well as what should have

been learned from the recent failures to reform other cultures that are profoundly different from our own) means that, aside from addressing our
own cultural problems, the best we can do is to resist the efforts of corporate interests to transform these other cultures into markets and sources of
cheap and easily exploitable labor.

Chapter Four

Community-Centered Approaches to Revitalizing the Commons

The suggestion that formal education can contribute to the revitalization of the commons is likely to elicit two reactions. Critics who view public schools and universities as sources of indoctrination into an industrial-dependent lifestyle are likely to argue that my suggestion is both naïve and contradictory—like suggesting that Congress will protect the interests of the people instead of the interests of corporations. These critics may be right on both counts. But my lack of total pessimism about the ability of public schools and universities to begin to address the deep cultural roots of the ecological crisis is expressed in my use of the word "can." What I am proposing is a possibility, not a certainty.

The other reaction to the suggestion about the role that education can play in revitalizing the commons is one that I have encountered whenever I have suggested that we can learn from cultures that have developed in ways that recognize the sustainable limits of their bioregions. The criticism, which interestingly enough is made by people with a university education, is that I am engaging in romantic thinking. As the proposal for revitalization of the commons will also be seen as challenging today's conventional wisdom that science, technology, and a market economy will overcome whatever problems and setbacks that seem to arise, it will be dismissed on the same grounds. The charge of romanticism will be supported by the formulaic arguments that we cannot go back to a simpler way of living, that progress is inevitable, and that if we don't promote consumerism people will be unable to earn a living.

The problem of romantic thinking does exist, but the charge of romantic thinking has been misdirected. Any discussion of the commons, particularly when it comes to making specific recommendations, must always take account of the unique characteristics of the bioregion as well as the cultural practices and beliefs of its inhabitants. If we understand romanticism as avoiding the realities of a culture's everyday environmental practices, as assuming that words such as "emancipation," "freedom," and "democracy" have a magical and universally transforming power, and as assuming that all of the world's cultures are waiting to be liberated and transformed in ways that reflect the Western reformers' way of thinking, then the charge of romantic thinking more appropriately applies to ethnocentric educational reformers such as John Dewey, Paulo Freire, and their many followers. On the other hand, a theory that takes account of cultural differences and the evidence of environmental degradation is not the expression of romantic, escapist thinking. Quite the opposite!

The educational theorists who assume that there is only one true approach to knowledge (experimental inquiry for Dewey, and critical reflection for Freire and his followers) operate in the realm of context-free theory—and thus are the true romantics. But their romanticism, which they do not recognize, also serves to support the neo-liberal ideology that is used to justify economic and technological globalization. That is, their romanticism is not the harmless word games of educational reformers who envision a better world. As we are now witnessing, the promotion of their theories of constructivist learning (now called "transformative learning") in Western and non-Western countries contributes to undermining cultural diversity and what remains of the local commons.

Ignoring the rapid changes occurring in natural systems as well as how these changes are affecting the health and prospects for a better quality of life for much of the world's population is also a characteristic of romantic thinking. Similarly, ignoring how the automation of the workplace and the outsourcing of jobs to regions of the world where wages are lower contributes to unemployment, while also failing to consider what the alternatives are to a money-dependent lifestyle, is also the expression of escapist, romantic thinking. The logic of capitalism requires that more labor-saving technologies be introduced, which means there is a corresponding drive to reduce the need for workers—a drive that is being accelerated as the burden of providing health care insurance and pensions for workers is also increasing at a rapid rate. Given these trends, the only realistic alternative is to consider the characteristics of communities that are less dependent upon consumerism; that is, communities that have maintained a more intelligent balance between market-oriented activities and other cultural values and practices. Perhaps a better way to represent this distinction is to understand the balance as between the monetized and nonmonetized activities and relationships within communities.

Any consideration of how different cultures balance the monetized and nonmonetized aspects of daily life involves considering the nature and importance of revitalizing the commons. The myth of endless technological progress and equally endless advances in the capacity to consume is coming up against the realities of global warming, depleted fisheries, shortage of potable water, and toxic contamination that is undermining the diversity of species—including human health. It is also being challenged by cultures that recognize the false promises inherent in the Western approach to development. While the rejection of Western culture does not always represent a higher standard of social justice and environmental responsibility, it nevertheless should be taken as further evidence that we need to rethink the wisdom of promoting the globalization of Western industrial-based culture.

The case I want to make here is that there is wisdom in the diverse cultural approaches to sustaining the commons. Furthermore there is wisdom in recognizing that the cultural practices and values that contribute to the viability of the commons do not have to be invented, but already exist—often in attenuated form. Indeed, many of the practices and values are so much a taken-for-granted aspect of community life that they go unnoticed. The wisdom we need to be clearer about, and this is where education "can" but not necessarily will play a constructive role, is in understanding how these nonmonetized activities and relationships not only represent an alternative to an environmentally destructive lifestyle we have been indoctrinated to pursue, but are the source of a more meaningful and fulfilling existence.

As mentioned earlier, automation and, now, the economic logic of globalization have reduced the number of workers in agriculture, government, and social services. Increasingly, white-collar jobs are now being outsourced to Third World countries. While work in an industrial setting has many drawbacks, it nevertheless enables people to pay their bills and to keep food on the table. With the disappearance of jobs as factories are relocated overseas, the ability to meet these basic needs becomes increasingly threatened. Over a three-year period, nearly 3 million jobs have been lost through downsizing, foreign competition, and the moving of factories to overseas locations. The state of Ohio, for example, lost over 160,000 factory jobs. The experience of workers in Canton, Ohio is all too typical of what is happening to workers across America. The personal experience of losing a job that was thought to be the basis of economic security over a lifetime, the uncertainties about the future, the anger, and the decline into poverty as bills go unpaid are now common among both blue-and white-collar workers. The 55-year-old tool-and-die worker who lost his job when the Hoover vacuum factory was moved from Canton to overseas, as well as the 54-year-old woman who, as a metallurgical technician, joined the ranks of the unemployed when Republic Steel closed down, typify the modern double bind where everyday life is dependent upon the industrial mode of production that is now disappearing in the United States. In too many instances the educational experiences of the growing newly unemployed left them with no understanding of the alternatives to a factory job. For many the prospects for employment in other fields are further diminished by age-related discrimination—even when other work opportunities become available. The immediate challenge facing these people whose world has suddenly been turned upside down is in meeting their house payments, paying for their children's education, avoiding illnesses that will force them deeper into debt, and in becoming depressed in ways that erode their self-confidence and self-esteem.

The slogans offered by today's educational reformers, which range from recommending that the curriculum be based on the great thinkers of the West to the romantic proposal that students should be encouraged to construct their own knowledge and values, are totally irrelevant to workers whose source of income and central focus in life has disappeared. The slogans of the latter group of educational reformers (the followers of Dewey, Freire, and Piaget—and the technology utopian thinkers) are the symbolic version of the Trojan Horse when they are promoted as the basis of educational reform in Third World countries where sweatshops are set up by Western corporations. For the unemployed workers these slogans are little more than being given Cool Whip on white bread.

What is missing in the education of the millions of the newly unemployed, and in the media accounts of their increasingly desperate lives, is the knowledge of how to live less consumer- and thus less industrial work-dependent lives. The focus in our educational institutions continues to be on the forms of knowledge and values that support the monetized aspects of daily life, while the nonmonetized possibilities continue to be ignored. The average student graduates from public schools and universities with so little knowledge of the nonmonetized possibilities within communities that, if asked, responds with either a blank stare or thinks that they have yet to be invented. While continually being undermined by the forces striving to turn every aspect of community and personal life into a market opportunity, there are many nonmonetized activities and forms of knowledge that exist, often in a highly attenuated condition, in most communities. As they have been relegated to low status by the industrial mentality that has enclosed much of the educational process, they receive almost no attention in our educational institutions that are bent on the promotion of new technologies, and the reinforcing of a form of individualism that wants to exist on the cusp of progress—which means buying the latest consumer fad.

The exporting (colonization) of the industrial culture is problematic for a number of reasons. The worldwide promotion of consumerism undermines the intergenerational knowledge that represents what remains of community self-sufficiency. It also further degrades the environment and contributes to the spread of industrial/environmentally related health problems. Thus, while I will focus here on the revitalization of the commons in Western cultures, it should be kept in mind that efforts to revitalize the commons in non-Western cultures should also be a primary concern. The differences in how the commons are understood in Western and non-Western cultures should not lead to ignoring that the process of enclosure is essentially the same: namely, the monetizing of more aspects of daily life.

REVITALIZING THE COMMONS
IN WESTERN CULTURES

One of the ironies that characterizes the increasing economic insecurity that many more people are facing is that they continue to drive cars and trucks that are grossly inefficient. They also continue to eat processed foods that are less nutritious and more expensive than home-prepared meals that utilize basic ingredients. That is, their lifestyle continues to be governed by the assumptions and habits that serve the interests of corporations even as these corporations pursue policies that are expanding the ranks of the unemployed and underpaid. A second irony is that the increasing number of unemployed and homeless, as well as the people nearing retirement who are witnessing the reduction in and even disappearance of their pension funds, are largely unaware of the resources and possibilities of the commons that represent the nonmonetized networks within their community.

In making the argument that revitalizing the commons, which would involve more widespread involvement of people in the nonmonetized activities and mutual support systems in the community, it should be kept in mind that I am not advocating that more people should be unemployed. The issues at stake here are more complicated than that, and they can only be understood by avoiding the simplistic thinking that relies upon dichotomous categories and slogans. The long history of labor strife, which has resulted in a number of gains for workers, has until recently marginalized any concern about the adverse impact of the industrial mode of production and consumption on the environment. This focus on improving working conditions also led to ignoring how industrial culture requires the destruction of the networks of self-reliance within communities, and undermines cultural diversity. What was important to critics and reformers was that more people should have jobs that paid a living wage, and that they be able to work in safe and humane conditions. But the very foundations of the industrial culture are now undergoing a basic change while, at the same time, requiring that people remain dependent upon consumerism to meet most aspects of daily life. The most basic change is that the new computer-based technologies are reducing the need for workers. Whether these new computer-driven technologies are less environmentally destructive is highly problematic, especially when we consider the toxic chemicals used in their manufacturing process and their subsequent release into the environment. But the destructive impact on the lives of millions of people who still live by the myths that sustained the early development and, now, the current spread of industrial culture is more evident—especially when we consider the amount of drugs that Americans require to stabilize their lives.

The radical change that is now needed is to de-emphasize the connection between work and money. The emerging post-market culture in the West, which is being ushered in by the growing ranks of the unemployed, requires a different understanding of work—what could be called a postindustrial way to think about work. And this, in turn, will require a post-market way of thinking about wealth. Understanding work as participation in community activities that range from volunteerism in projects that address the needs of the homeless and the elderly to mentoring youth and restoring natural systems has a number of immediate benefits. For example, understanding work as a form of community service that involves doing something that is meaningful and constructive in terms of the lives of others reduces the need to consume. That is, it helps to bring into perspective that the quality of everyday life, and one's sense of self-worth, are not dependent upon consumerism. People may even come to realize that the quality of their lives has been vastly improved over being caught in the cycle of doing unfulfilling work in order to pay the bills accumulated by keeping up with the latest consumer trends. In short, they may come to realize that they can live more meaningful lives by being less dependent upon a money economy.

This view of work as participating in community-renewal activities certainly will not support the mortgage payment on a house with a three-car garage that is part of the "super-sizing" trend that represents the latest phase in the development of our industrial culture. However, as Jeremy Rifkin points out, it is a trend that is taking hold in countries where unemployment is becoming more widespread—and in Third World countries where unemployment has been the legacy of the West's false promises. In France, for example, the government pays a monthly salary to the approximately 350,000 men and women who work in nonprofit community-centered activities. In Great Britain there are nearly a third of a million voluntary organizations that now account for close to 4 percent of the country's gross national product. Japan also has vast networks of voluntary associations that continue to expand as market-related work continues to decline. The number of volunteer organizations is also increasing in other parts of the world. Brazil, for example, has more than 100,000 community-based organizations that are engaged in a variety of advocacy, educational, and health care efforts among the poorest segment of the population. Similar groups in other South American countries are addressing the needs currently ignored by corporations and governments by providing child care centers, food and transportation cooperatives, and basic services such as garbage removal and improving the availability of safe drinking water.

The scope of volunteerism and work in the nonprofit sectors of American communities often escapes notice as it is treated as the largely invisible economy—except during the yearly drive for contributions for such organizations as the United Way. The following summary of the activities that strengthens the commons, and that provides nonindustrial forms of work, includes many of the networks of mutual support that exist in varying degrees in our own communities.

According to Rifkin, they run the gamut

from social services to health care, education and research, the arts, religion, and advocacy. Community service organizations assist the elderly and handicapped, the mentally ill, disadvantaged youth, the homeless and the indigent. Volunteers renovate dilapidated apartments and build new low-income housing. Tens of thousands of Americans volunteer their services in public-supported hospitals and clinics, taking care of patients, including victims of AIDS. Thousands more serve as foster parents, or as big brothers and sisters for orphaned children. Some provide counseling for runaway and troubled youth. Others are tutors, recruited into the campaign to eliminate illiteracy. Americans assist in day-care centers and after-school programs. They prepare and deliver meals to the poor. A growing number of Americans volunteer in crisis centers, helping rape victims and the victims of spouse and child abuse. Thousands volunteer their time staffing public shelters and distributing clothes to the needy. Many Americans are involved in self-help programs like Alcoholics Anonymous, and in drug rehabilitation programs. Professionals—lawyers, doctors, executives—donate their services to voluntary organizations. Millions of Americans volunteer their time to various environmental efforts, including recycling activities, conservation programs, antipollution campaigns, and animal protection work. Others work for advocacy organizations attempting to redress grievances and change public perceptions and laws. Hundreds of thousands of Americans give their time to the arts—participating in local theater groups, choirs, and orchestras. Volunteers often assist municipal governments, serving as volunteer firefighters or donating time to crime prevention work and disaster relief. (1996: 240)

As this list indicates, there are plenty of work opportunities that have not been eliminated by automation and the outsourcing of jobs to Third World countries. The problem is that recent federal governments, while giving lip service to the importance of this sector of the economy, have chosen instead to give massive subsidies to corporations seeking to expand their markets around the world. They have also used the work of the community service groups as an excuse for reducing federal funding of public education, health programs, housing, transportation, and other basic services that are especially critical to the lives of the poor and marginalized citizens. Providing government support so that many of the volunteer services and activities that Rifkin lists can provide a living wage will require a radical change in the public's understanding of what the priorities of the government should be.

Basically, the distinction between priorities currently comes down to whether the government will use the people's taxes to support military interventions in countries where corporate interests are being threatened or to support the efforts of community-based groups working to improve the quality of the lives of citizens—and to ensuring that the environment will be able to sustain the same quality of life for future generations. Support that contributes to renewing the commons could take the form of tax breaks for workers who volunteer their time and talents. Other possibilities include direct subsidies that translate into a living wage for community service workers, and a guaranteed wage for all citizens. The enclosure of the democratic process that has been accelerating in recent years as politicians become more dependent upon the financial support of corporations and the super-rich is going to make any serious reconsideration of our society's priorities especially difficult to achieve. However, as unemployment reaches further into the middle class, a basic change may become inevitable.

While we wait for the political miracle of the century, the on-the-ground reality persists. Indeed, the crisis deepens daily as corporations announce the layoffs of a significant percentage of their work force—all in the name of increasing profits and their competitiveness. So the problem remains: What do the laid-off workers do with their time and talents? And the problem that transcends the immediate plight of the unemployed remains: namely, what can be done to revitalize the commons in order to ensure that a degraded environment is not the legacy we leave to future generations? Indeed, the problem that supercedes all others is the decline in the self-renewing capacity of the natural systems that all life depends upon. As pointed out earlier, the alternatives to the industrial culture do not have to be created anew, as they are already practiced in many American communities, and in the communities of other cultures. However, the suggestion that we can learn from other cultures requires making a clear distinction between learning and borrowing. I am definitely not suggesting the latter as it represents a further form of colonization of the culture that is being borrowed from while strengthening the myth that industrial culture is totally inclusive.

OTHER APPROACHES TO REVITALIZING THE COMMONS

While a basic pattern of thinking persists, especially among people with a university education, that represents the Western technologically based culture as more evolved than the indigenous cultures of North America, many of these indigenous cultures still have much to teach us about how to live in a sustainable relationship with non-human members of the commons. In suggesting that we can learn from indigenous cultures whose traditions of self-sufficiency have been undermined by generations of exploitation and racism, I am mindful that not all of these cultures are models of environmental stewardship, and that not all of them maintained peaceful relationships with their neighbors. The reliance of many of these cultures in more recent years on casino gambling as a means of meeting basic social needs in a money economy is understandable, if regrettable. In spite of this yielding to one of the worst characteristics of the dominant culture, many of these indigenous cultures still possess traditions of stewardship of the commons, with some of these ancient traditions even becoming more robust. Other traditions of stewardship are becoming more attenuated under the impact of the media, consumerism, an increasing reliance upon a money economy, and the Western model of schooling.

While the picture is mixed, there are diverse cultural traditions still carried on that we can learn from. It is important to emphasize again that there is a difference between learning from other cultures, and borrowing from them. The cultural traditions that seem particularly relevant to sustaining the commons include the following: an inclusive understanding of the spiritual universe, a long view of an intergenerationally connected existence, a way of experiencing place in a way that combines a complex knowledge of local ecosystems with the practice of moral reciprocity.

One of the cultural patterns shared but expressed differently by indigenous cultures across North America (including Central and South America) is the understanding that the commons (plants, animals, rivers, humans, etc.) are equal participants in the same spiritual universe. This profound sense of spiritual unity that binds together all the participants of the commons, and accounts for the diverse practices of moral reciprocity between humans and the non-human members of the commons, can be seen in the following statements. As Chief Standing Bear of the Lokata band of the Sioux summarized the spiritual, sacred unity of the commons:

> Kinship with all creatures of the earth, sky, water was a real and active principle. For the animal and bird world there existed a brotherly feeling that kept the Lakota safe among them and so close did some of the Lakotas come to their feathered and furred friends that in true brotherhood they spoke a common tongue. The old Lakota was wise. He knew that man's heart away from nature becomes hard; he knew that lack of respect for growing, living

things soon led to lack of respect for humans too. So he kept his youth close to its softening influence. (quoted in McLuhan 1971: 6)

A prominent medicine man of Standing Rock Reservation, Tatanka-ohitika (Brave Buffalo) put it this way: "When I was ten years of age I looked at the land and the rivers, the sky above, and the animals around me and could not fail to realize that they were made of some great power" (McLuhan, 16). Chief Joseph of the Nez Perce not only expressed the widely shared indigenous understanding that the commons should not be privately owned but also explained a basic relationship that modern ecologists are just now beginning to understand:

> The earth was created by the assistance of the sun, and it should be left as it was. . . . The country was made without lines of demarcation, and it was no man's business to divide it. . . . I see the whites all over the country gaining wealth, and see their desire to give us lands which are worthless. . . . The earth and myself are of one mind. The measure of the land and the measure of our bodies are the same. Say to us if you can say it, that you were sent by the Creative Power to talk to us. Perhaps you think the Creator sent you here to dispose of us as you see fit. If I thought you were sent by the Creator I might be induced to think you had the right to dispose of me. Do not misunderstand me, but understand me fully with reference to my affection for the land. I never said the land was mine to do with it as I chose. The one who has the right to dispose of it is the one who has created it. I claim a right to live on my land, and accord you the privilege to live on yours. (McLuhan: 54)

This spiritually inclusive way of understanding what is here being referred to as the commons led to the practice of interspecies communication that Gary Snyder brings out in the retelling of the story of "The Woman Who Married a Bear" (1990: 155–174). It also led to giving close attention to what the various members of the commons were communicating about their relationships, and where they were in their cycle of life—knowledge that was essential to the prospects of humans. For example, the way in which the Quechua of the Andes adapt their decisions about where to graze their animals on the basis of the egg-laying behavior of a local bird, which signals future changes in weather patterns—including availability of rain, is typical of this indigenous practice of learning from the interactive patterns of natural systems.

Another cultural pattern shared by indigenous cultures, and again variously expressed, is the long view of the life of the commons—and of human responsibility. Unlike the individually centered view of time that is learned in the West, indigenous cultures have an intergenerationally centered view of time. Red Jacket, in commenting on his own death, expressed concern about the prospects of the seventh unborn generation. This view of time where decisions are made in a way that takes into consideration the consequences for the seventh unborn generation was similarly expressed more recently in an interview that Oren Lyons, a chief of the Onondaga Nation, had with Bill Moyers. The long-range way of experiencing where one is in the cycle of time/life also includes giving special standing to the wisdom of elders. Among indigenous cultures, elders are important for a number of reasons: as carriers of the moral wisdom accumulated over generations of living within a specific place (bioregion), as a source of knowledge of sustainable practices that have been refined over generations of collective experience, and as keepers of the narratives that bridge generations by reinforcing the sense of a common origin and moral values.

The sense of being deeply rooted in the commons is also a characteristic of indigenous cultures across North America. Joseph Epes Brown summarizes the multiple dimensions of their knowledge of place—and their sense of connectedness:

> Native American experiences of place are infused with mythic themes. These express events of sacred time, which are as real now as at any other time. They are experienced through landmarks in each people's immediate natural environment. The events of animal beings, for example, which are communicated through oral traditions of myth or folklore, serve to grace, sanctify, explain, and interpret each detail of the land. Further, each being of nature, every particular form of the land, is experienced as the locus of qualitatively differentiated spirit beings, whose individual and collective presence sanctifies and gives meaning to the land in all its details and contours. Thus, it also gives meaning to the lives of people who cannot conceive of themselves as apart from the land. (1985: 51)

The importance of knowing the life cycles of the animals, plants, and other participants in the commons (bioregion), as well as treating them as sacred, leads to an emphasis being placed on cultural practices that are more attuned to the life-renewing characteristics of natural systems. This, in turn, leads to a profoundly different form of scientific knowledge. Unlike Western science, where the goal of acquiring knowledge is to achieve greater control over, and even to create substitutes for, natural processes, indigenous knowledge that leads to explanations, predictions, and the control of outcomes is governed by a deep sense of moral reciprocity and of the sacredness of natural processes. The sense of the sacred, which requires continual acknowledgment of nature's bountifulness and the experience of kinship with the life that must be taken in order to sustain human life, does not preclude close observation of natural processes. Indeed, the complex knowledge of plants, animals, weather patterns, and so forth, enabled indigenous cultures to survive in environments that the European settlers deemed uninhabitable. Accurate knowledge of the medicinal properties of plants, as well as the knowledge of the diversity of life cycles of the local ecosystems they depended upon for food and shelter, attest to their being close observers—and even to their ability to experiment in ways that were informed by the processes of nature.

The removal of indigenous cultures from the commons that were the source of their traditional knowledge and identity, as well as the impact of Western schooling and the media, have forced many indigenous cultures to adapt to the demands of a money economy by opening gambling casinos. This development, which might be interpreted as a way of taking revenge upon the Euro-American culture, is surely at odds with the traditional values and intergenerational knowledge of the indigenous cultures spread across North America. The transforming impact of this latest violation of traditional knowledge will only become fully understood as the younger generation reaches the age where they become leaders in their communities.

For the Anglo and Euro-Americans who face the incessant drive to enclose what remains of the commons, and who find that the twin forces of economic globalization and automation are reducing the availability of work, there is the question that is raised by the traditions of the indigenous cultures—even in their attenuated condition. That is, can the commons that the majority of Anglo and Euro-Americans depend upon be sustained if the key characteristics of the indigenous cultures are missing? Can the commons that are spread across North America sustain human life over the long run if the natural cycles of life are not experienced as sacred and interdependent—and if the daily practice of moral reciprocity and thanksgiving are absent? Can the commons survive if the long view of life, which is based on the renewing of intergenerational knowledge, is not part of the culture? The latter question can be framed in another way that brings out the total indifference to the commons that is at the center of current thinking about the direction that educational reform should take. Thus, the question becomes: can the commons be renewed if the younger generation is told that they should construct their own knowledge and determine their own values?

Just as the indigenous cultures, in their diversity, shared common practices in how they related to their environment, there is a similar mix of diversity and shared patterns among the Anglo and Euro-Americans who have a history of ambivalence toward the spread of industrial culture. These shared patterns include valuing the talents and craft knowledge of individuals, work that is not governed by the logic of industrial production and consumption, use of local materials, small-scale producers, and reliance on local markets, and the belief that work should contribute to the well-being of the community. The Shakers who built communities in New England and the Midwest exhibited a number of traits that are still carried forward by craftspeople who work in a variety of media: wood, glass, ceramics, weaving, and so forth. Work for the Shakers was part of their spiritual discipline. This tradition is still carried on by women and men who have deliberately kept themselves separate from the industrial approach to production. The key elements of their craft include a deep understanding of the materials they work with, aesthetic judgment, and a highly developed level of execution. These elements, for example, characterize the furniture designed and made by Michael Puryear, an African American who possesses a wide knowledge of cultural approaches to design, but who brings his own sense of aesthetic judgment to these diverse traditions. While Puryear exhibits his work at major design shows, and has achieved national recognition as a master craftsperson, nearly every community in America has people who work with wood and other materials in ways that correspond to the Shakers' belief that working with one's hands is a sacred act. It is also an act of political resistance to the industrial mode of production that is spreading to regions of the world where the idea of modernization has taken hold.

The economy of the commons is best expressed in the various small-scale producers, such as small coastal canneries where the tuna is hand-filleted and hand-packed, the organic farms that provide safe and nourishing produce for the local market, the weavers who combine personal skill and aesthetic judgment with selling locally during the holiday seasons, the local cabinet or furniture maker, and so forth. Unlike the worker in a factory setting, these varied approaches to work strengthen the face-to-face and often economically interdependent networks within the community.

This small-scale and more mutually reliant approach to work is also less environmentally destructive. Workers who are place-based both in terms of self-identity and economic interdependence are far less likely to rely upon toxic chemicals than is the current case with factories where decisions about production goals, and the technologies that will meet them, are set by corporate heads who are far removed from the environmental havoc that too often results from their decisions.

Among the many other benefits of the small-scale and community-oriented producer there are two others that deserve special mention. For the millions of Americans who now find themselves unemployed and with time on their hands, the development of a craft that often involves participating in a larger network of people with similar interests represents an alternative to the depression and the health-destroying resentment that too often accompany the sense of being discarded and labeled as useless by the company that has moved its production process to an overseas site. A second benefit of small-scale community-centered production is that it often leads to a reprioritizing of personal values where the need to consume becomes less important. A strong case can be made that it is the lack of personal meaningfulness and sense of isolation from deep interpersonal relationships that too often characterizes today's modern workplace that leads to the hyper-consumerism that, in turn, requires working longer hours, often at several jobs, in order to pay the bills.

The criticism is likely to be made that the unemployed lack the resources to purchase the tools and other equipment necessary to centering their lives in some craft tradition that could become the source of their livelihood. Those who make this criticism do not understand another characteristic of the people who have developed lives of mutual interdependence. That is, as these craftspeople, artists, volunteers, mentors, master gardeners, and so forth, are sought out the wherewithal for participating in the economy of the commons will become clearer. Apprenticeships will be discovered, as well as information about where the equipment for the novice can be acquired at a lower cost—or is available on a loan basis. In terms of woodworking, many communities have a high school that is equipped with the necessary tools that can be used by the community in the evening. The problem is not the inaccessible nature of the tools, mentors, and mutual support systems, but the conditioning to the industrial approach to work that leaves the unemployed worker ignorant of the community-centered possibilities. The media emphasis on consumerism, which keeps the workers tied to the cycle of working in order to purchase the latest fad, and the indoctrination to the values and thought patterns of industrial culture that are promoted by public schools and universities, are also responsible for unemployed workers not recognizing the alternative possibilities within their communities.

The industrialization of agriculture represents yet another example of enclosure that is having a devastating impact on the environment—and on the ability of the traditional small-scale farmer to stay on the land. Since World War II, more than 15 million men and women have left farming in the United States. With NAFTA and the American government's policy of giving massive subsidies to agri-businesses, the small-scale farmers in Mexico and other Third World countries are also being driven off the land that had been the central feature of their culture for hundreds of years. It now seems that genetically engineered seeds, the use of chemicals and ever-larger farm machinery, and the use of computers represent an irreversible trend that the rest of the world must follow. In spite of what appears as overwhelming odds that resistance will be futile, and the massive efforts of the media to represent agri-business as the only way to feed the world's growing population, the small-scale farmers in India, Peru, and other Third World countries continue to resist—and have had some successes.

Here at home the alternatives to the industrialization of agriculture are being promoted by groups such as the Land Institute in Salinas, Kansas, which is working to preserve the genetic diversity of edible plants and the recovery of the tall-grass prairie, and the organic farmers who have started a trend that even the supermarkets can no longer ignore. The early Shakers modeled how small-scale farming could be both productive and ecologically sustainable. Today, religious groups such as the Amish and Mennonites continue to demonstrate the long-term and multiple advantages of small-scale farming. In addition to introducing such early sound agricultural practices as crop rotation, they continue to exhibit a deep understanding of the need to assess technological decisions in terms of other concerns and values such as the destructive impact of heavy machinery on the soil, the possible contamination of the groundwater, the need to avoid the huge burden of debt that accompanies the supposedly labor saving megafarm equipment, and the spiritual requirement of being stewards of the land. Again, in suggesting that we can learn from these groups about what constitutes the appropriate size of a farm, and how their communal practices represent examples of how cultural and natural systems can be a source of mutual nurturance, it must be kept in mind that I am not suggesting that everyone should join their communities. Rather, other cultural groups can learn from them just as they can learn from the many aspects of indigenous cultures without engaging in cultural appropriation. The challenge is for the other cultural groups, especially the dominant Anglo and Euro-American culture, to find within their own traditions the basis for achieving the sustainable practices that have been carried on by the indigenous and other nonindustrially oriented cultural groups.

Just as the people in the various crafts find dignity and self-expression in working with their hands, the successful small-scale farmers such as the Amish, Mennonites, and the Quechua (to cite a Third World example) have also associated hand labor with the higher values. Work in industrial settings, whether in the factory or in following behind a massive piece of farm machinery, is oppressive in a variety of ways, including being repetitive, enforcing a pace of work that is dictated by the machine, often working in a chemically toxic environment, and largely eliminating the social dimensions of work that are not hierarchically organized. The incessant drive to automate work and to send assembly plants to Third World locations is motivated more by the desire for higher profits than the stultifying nature of factory work. Again, it needs to be emphasized that the alternative to the alienating nature of the industrial mode of production, and to the increasing insecurity caused by the low wages being paid in Third World countries, will require a radical change in how work has come to be understood in the dominant culture. That is, we will need to make a basic shift from thinking that all work is alienating and thus in need of being replaced by further automation to thinking within one of the craft traditions of work.

Just as the African-American communities in the east-side of Detroit have made urban agriculture an important aspect of their efforts to achieve greater local self-sufficiency, urban agriculture is taking hold in other urban settings such as Philadelphia, Chicago, Boston, and New York City—as well as in smaller cities across the country. While some gardens are now being planted on rooftops, the majority involve transforming vacant lots into community gardens. The decline in the population of Philadelphia, for example, has led to an increased number of vacant lots as abandoned houses have been torn down. These lots have been turned into over 500 community gardens that involve nearly 3,000 families. Gardens planted on land that has been taken over by the local community represent, in effect, reversing the process of enclosure.

In addition to providing nourishing vegetables, the community gardens serve to connect the youth with the older members of the community. They also strengthen important ethnic traditions. The growing of vegetables associated with ethnic traditions, as well as the preparation and customs governing the sharing of a meal, are examples of resistance to the industrially prepared foods that are now contributing to the alienation between generations—and thus to undermining cultural diversity. The ethnic community gardens in Philadelphia can also be understood as sites of affirmation that nourish both bodies and intergenerationally connected identities. For example, the gardens in African-American neighborhoods include peanuts and collards, while the Korean gardens grow peppers, huge radishes, and greens. In Puerto Rican neighborhoods the gardens include pigeon peas and even bananas. Filipino and Southern Italian gardens include the vegetables found in their respective traditional cultures.

Urban agriculture is being adopted in North and South Africa, South America, Europe, and Asia. Cuba is a particularly important example of how urban agriculture contributes to greater self-sufficiency. The shift from reliance on imported food to agricultural self-reliance was not driven by ideology, but by the collapse of the monocrop and chemical-intensive approach to agriculture that resulted from disintegration of the socialist bloc in late 1989. The decision to replace the industrial approach to agriculture with one that promoted small urban gardens based on appropriate ecologically informed technologies has resulted in greater self-reliance in food production. For example, 90 percent of the fresh vegetables consumed in Havana are grown in small urban gardens.

In addition to contributing to greater self-sufficiency, which in itself is a form of resistance to economic and technological globalization, urban agriculture helps to renew the intergenerational knowledge of the relationship between seeds, proper care of the soil, and nourishment. And the renewing of the knowledge of these fundamental relationships is central to Edmund Burke's observation about the importance of community as "a partnership between those who are living, those who are dead, and those who are to be born" (1962: 140). To recall an earlier discussion, Cornel West makes a similar statement when he writes about how an industrial-based culture contributes to "the loss of ties at birth of ascending and descending generations, a loss of ties to both predecessor and progeny (1993: 149). What is overlooked by liberal social and educational reformers who emphasize the importance of emancipating people from their cultural traditions so that they can live in a world that is in a constant state of change (a vision they share with the promoters of the industrial culture) is that the intergenerational knowledge of how to grow and prepare food in urban settings is one of the more promising expressions of resistance to the industrial market, as well as to the educational and political forces that are undermining the diversity of cultural languages and thus the collective memories of how to sustain the commons.

There are many other examples of how the globalization of industrial culture is being resisted at the local level. Two especially noteworthy examples are the creation of local currencies and barter systems, and the growing practice of adopting voluntary simplicity as a personal lifestyle. Local currencies, what are being called "local exchange trading systems" (LETS), take different forms, from the use of community-issued scrip that has an agreed-upon exchange value to barter systems and the exchange of skills. The use of LETS can now be found in communities across the United States, Canada, Australia, and Great Britain. Joel Russ, the co-founder of a LETS association in British Columbia, summarizes how the use of local currency and other exchange systems strengthens the interdependence within the community:

A problem with conventional money is that (as part of the vast international market system) it tends to flow to where it makes the most money—usually to the biggest cities, the trade and industrial centers, a good share of it finally coursing into and through the bank accounts of very wealthy weapons and oil peddlers. Such, after all, is the immense scope of The System. But most of us live closer to the other end of the scale, and we voluntary simplicists can often feel we have too little money for our needs. A LET System keeps local energy local, rather than pouring it (in dollar-bill form) out of the community. LETS thus supports a truly local economy. Those who believe in reducing their participation in the standard currency system, thereby contributing to reducing The System's pressure on natural systems, find LETS participation a meaningful ecological gesture. (Meeker-Lowry 1996: 449–450)

Local currencies, in effect, are based on face-to-face relationships that require mutual consent. Thus, they strengthen decision-making that takes account of the common good. Local exchange systems, which are not accepted as legitimate currency in the megastores that can only pay their bills by using conventional currency, also strengthen local producers who are less likely to rely upon an industrial system of production. Another advantage of local exchange systems is that they provide a greater margin of independence from the megastores, with their industrially produced goods—including processed foods. This independence, in turn, leads to less wasteful consumerism and thus to a smaller adverse impact on the environment.

What needs to be understood about the varied approaches to the use of local exchange systems is that with few exceptions it is impossible to live in a way that is entirely free of the need for an income in the form of the national currency. We are so dependent upon modern technologies for health care, building materials, communication, and so forth, that there are always needs that can only be met by participating in the larger economic system. It is therefore important to recognize that while local exchange systems are vital to strengthening the commons, and that they represent forms of resistance to the colonizing power of industrial culture, they reduce rather than eliminate total dependence on the industrial mode of production and consumption. Even the Amish, for all of their achievements in attaining a high degree of self-sufficiency, still need to earn an income in order to pay for the telephone that is often located down by the road, and to pay for the gasoline that is used in their limited range of farm machinery.

Another development that strengthens the commons is what is being called "voluntary simplicity." The bible of this movement, which is spreading among people who are consciously avoiding being trapped in the consumer culture of the middle class, is *Your Money or Your Life* (1992), by Joe Dominguez and Vicki Robin. Dominguez and Robin highlight the fears, frustrations, and stresses that accompany the relentless drive to consume at the level the media represents as the standard of success in American society. Having held up a mirror that readers can recognize themselves in, the authors then identify the simple steps that individuals can take to reduce their need for money while at the same time achieving greater self-development and satisfaction. These common-sense steps to a life of voluntary simplicity include: "Stop trying to impress people," "Don't go shopping" (which leads to impulse buying), "Live within your means," "Take care of what you have," "Wear it out," "Do it yourself," "Anticipate your needs," " Research value, quality, durability, and multiple use," "Get it for less," and "Buy it used" (171–181).

In addition to restating this Benjamin Franklin type of wisdom of how to live full and socially meaningful lives, Dominguez and Robin urge that one of the keys to a life of voluntary simplicity is to redefine work so that it is no longer equated with paid employment. As they put it:

> Breaking the link between work and wages has as much power in our lives as the recognition that money is simply "something we trade our life energy for." Money is our life energy; it takes its value not from external definitions but from what we invest in it. Similarly, paid employment takes its only *intrinsic* value from the fact that we are paid to do it. Everything else we do is an expression of who we are, not what we must to do out of economic necessity. By breaking the link we regain quality, values and self-worth as our bottom line. By breaking the link we can redefine work simply as whatever we do in alignment with our purpose in life. By breaking the link we get our life back. (231)

The art of learning to live in ways that are less dependent upon *earning* a living has a direct relationship to a revitalized commons. In addition to reducing the need to turn more of the natural environment into consumer products and services, and eventually into toxic waste and garbage that is overwhelming our ability to dispose of it, reducing the need to work frees up time for participating in the cultural aspects of the commons—conversations with family and friends, contributing to the arts, participating in sports, gardening, volunteering in ways that help others, developing a craft, mentoring and being mentored, and so forth.

A final point needs to be made about understanding the radical realignment of values and thinking that voluntary simplicity requires: namely, that continued automation and the outsourcing of work to low-wage regions of the world are forcing more people to abandon the American dream of a money-dependent lifestyle. The people who are voluntarily practicing a simpler and thus less consumer-dependent lifestyle are demonstrating that we can live fuller and more satisfying lives on less money that what most Americans have been indoctrinated to think is possible. The other fact of life is that the environment does not negotiate with us when it is being overstressed and degraded in ways that alter its self-renewing capacity. Changes in climate, the lack of potable water and the drying up of aquifers, and the disappearance of fish stocks are proving to be beyond what the industrial culture can manage or compensate for. Yet, instead of awakening from the mesmerizing power of the myths that underlie the West's industrial culture, the promoters and chief economic opportunists are now extending the process of enclosure to include the gene lines of plants and animals. And some of its latest visionaries are working to create a future occupied only by robots and computers that are networked together. For them the commons will be transformed into a constant flow of information passing between computers that will design the next generation of computers, repair themselves, and overcome the human problem of mortality by constantly backing up their data bases (Moravec 1988, and Kurzweil 1999).

As the current efforts to extend the process of enclosure to the biological basis of life and thus to incorporate it into the industrial process, as well as the efforts to replace humans with computer-based technologies and to justify this vision of the future on the basis that it is part of the evolutionary process, it is necessary to acknowledge the nature and the importance of the ideologies that represent a further threat to what remains of the commons. These ideologies need to be understood if we are to avoid the double bind of promoting educational reforms that perpetuate the values and patterns of thinking that, in the name of a sustainable future, were and continue to be the basis of the industrial culture that has already exceeded the self-renewing capacity of natural systems.

Chapter Five

Understanding the Commons within the Context of Contemporary Ideologies

It is important that the everyday life in the world's diverse commons be understood within the context of current ideological orientations such as liberalism, conservatism (as currently misused in the press and by politicians), and the ideology that is being represented as serving as a bridge between the two—that is, libertarianism. Understanding the basic differences between the cultural assumptions and values that influence everyday life in the commons, which varies between cultures, as well as the current reliance on different interpretations of classical liberal ideas as a guide to both domestic and international governmental policies, is especially important if we are to recognize the different ways in which the world's commons are being threatened. Among the characteristics shared by the different interpretations of classical liberal thinking—social justice liberals, market liberals, "free-market conservatives," and libertarians—is that they all are represented as a blueprint for achieving a better future for humankind. This justification, which is intended to put them beyond the realm of criticism, hides their true purpose—which is to universalize the most ecologically and culturally destructive aspects of Western culture.

I argue in *Mindful Conservatism: Rethinking the Ideological and Educational Basis of an Ecologically Sustainable Future* (2003) that the need today, given the rate of technological change and the incessant intrusion of market forces into every aspect of daily life, is to be mindful (that is, reflective) about which traditions are essential to the health of the commons, and which traditions carry forward socially unjust and ecologically destructive practices. Thus it is important to clarify why the use of the phrase "mindful conservatism" needs to be considered as profoundly different from the ideological agendas of such so-called conservatives as

Rush Limbaugh and President George W. Bush, from liberal social and educational reformers such as Paulo Freire and Moacir Gadotti, as well as from the political theorists who are attempting to promote libertarianism as the alternative to the all-controlling nature of the state.

There are Western thinkers who have articulated basic conservative guidelines that support a more culturally and ecologically informed interpretation of mindful conservatism. For example, Edmund Burke's argument about the current generation's responsibility for ensuring that the genuine achievements of the past be carried forward and renewed, as well as his emphasis on the need for each generation to live in ways that do not diminish the prospects of future generations, represents a basic wisdom shared by many of the world's cultures. Indeed, the cultural practice of honoring one's ancestors, which is widespread in many regions of the world where the West's notion of the autonomous individual has not taken hold, exhibits the Burkean sensitivity to the intergenerationally connected nature of human life. The wisdom of indigenous cultures spread across North, Central, and South America that decisions must take account of the seventh unborn generation, as well as cultures that project their responsibility even further into the future, is also part of this conserving tradition.

The conservative nature of both the cultural and natural systems is far more deeply rooted than Burke's reflections on the nature of intergenerational responsibility and his well-founded criticisms of the emerging myth that equates change with social progress. However, before examining the dominant Western ideologies that have their origins in the abstract ideas of political philosophers and theorists, it is necessary to identify the different ways in which cultures as well as natural systems are inherently conserving in nature. This seemingly sweeping generalization also applies to cultures based on Western assumptions that equate change with progress, the empowerment of the individual with greater autonomy, and in other ways assume that life can be lived more fully if all traditions are rejected. But the unexamined assumptions that underlie the various interpretations of classical liberal ideas and everyday experience are not the same—even for political theorists. Even though the "educated" elites within the West that correctly represent the industrial, scientifically based culture as in a constant state of change, the underlying assumptions that lead them to equate change with progress are intergenerationally conserved by public schools, universities, and the practices of corporations.

When E. O. Wilson urges the world's cultures to abandon their ancient religions in order to adopt the Western scientists' account of how natural and cultural systems evolved over the last 14 billion years (1998: 264–265), he is exhibiting the same ignorance about the multiple ways in which cultures conserve their traditions that is shared by other Western theorists who have substituted print-based and thus abstract knowledge for a deep understanding of the taken-for-granted patterns of experience within their own as well as in other cultures. For example, when Moacir Gadotti urges the entire world to adopt a "planetary consciousness" that is to be acquired through the exploration of the individual's inner world, and when Francis Crick announces that scientists are on the verge of explaining the genetic basis of consciousness that leads to exceptional talent of the mathematician and musician, and when thousands of other Western thinkers make similar universal statements, we are witnessing the same mix of Western hubris and cultural ignorance that can be traced back to the earliest Western philosophers—a tradition that still is largely insulated from critical examination.

The following explanation of the many ways in which biological and cultural processes are inherently conserving in nature should not be interpreted as affirming every pattern that is reproduced over the generations. That is, the need is to understand how biological and cultural patterns reproduce themselves, how these conserving patterns undergo minor changes in response to internal and external forces, as well as how they represent the dominant characteristic of life-forming and culture sustaining processes. Understanding these conservative patterns, from how the DNA carries forward (conserves) the instructions for the formation of cells and organs, and how they function in support of the larger biological system, as well as how a culture reproduces (conserves) its distinctive patterns of thinking and values, is essential to clarifying how the different interpretations of liberalism in the West misrepresent the nature of conservatism. In effect, what is being proposed here is that the core misunderstandings encoded and carried forward in the words "liberalism," "conservatism," and "libertarianism" can be traced to the failure to understand the conserving processes in the natural and cultural systems that support a sustainable commons.

As I have written about the inherently conserving nature of intergenerationally connected cultures (1995, 2001, 2003, 2004), I will introduce Guillermo Bonfil Batalla's explanation of what is involved in being a

member of a culture. His major concern is to explain to Western thinkers
that the ancient cultures of Mesoamerica are still viable—indeed, that they
are in a period of self-regeneration and thus consciously resisting the pressures of Western development. But his explanation of what each generation learns from membership in a culture can be applied to other cultures
where the patterns and deeply held assumptions differ widely. As he puts
it, as a member of culture

> We learn how to do things, to do the kind of work that is done here, to inter-
> pret the natural world and its expressions, to find ways of confronting
> problems, to name things. Along with this we also receive values: what is
> right and wrong, what is desirable and what is not, what is permitted
> and what is forbidden, what should be—the relative value of all acts and
> things. One generation transmits to those that follow the codes that allow
> communication and mutual understanding. It transmits a particular language
> that expresses the vision of the world and the ideas created by the group
> throughout its history. Also transmitted are the particular gestures, tones
> of voice, ways of looking, and attitudes that have meaning for us, and
> often for us alone. At a deeper level a spectrum of sentiments are also trans-
> mitted. Because they are shared, they allow us to participate, to accept,
> and to believe. Without them personal relations and collective effort would
> be impossible. All this is culture, and each generation receives it enriched
> by the effort and the imagination of those who went before. As each gen-
> eration is shaped within the culture, it in turn helps to enrich that culture.
> (1996: 21)

What needs to be added to his explanation is that the symbolic aspects of
the culture, which influence all the dimensions of culture that Batalla
describes, are rooted in the mythopoetic narratives of the culture—and in
powerful evocative experiences such as the West's fascination with mechanical processes that became the early basis of Western science and industrial
mode of production. That is, a culture's symbolic world is derived from its
stories of creation, which can be seen in the influence that the Book of Genesis has had on the West's tradition of patriarchy, anthropocentrism, and
individual accountability. We can see in the mythopoetic narratives (cosmo-
vision, creation stories, etc.) of such cultures as the Hopi, Quechua, Maori,
as well as in the major religious traditions of Buddhism, Hinduism, Confucianism, and Islam, the basic assumptions that govern their moral codes,
systems of decision-making, approaches to built environments, healing
practices, ways of understanding human/nature relationships, and so on.

The many Western thinkers who have been indoctrinated with abstract explanations of conservatism and liberalism have a proclivity to think that traditions are static and thus stand in the way of progress. The more unreflective liberals who have reduced critical reflection to a rigid formula that is dependent upon the cultural myth of progress go even further by claiming that conservatism stands for the preservation of wealth, special privileges, and self-serving political power. However, their biggest error is in equating conservatism with the global spread of the West's industrial culture. In the case of many cultures, power and wealth are unevenly distributed, and horrendous practices such as slavery (now estimated to be 25 million people) and other forms of economic exploitation are still practiced. These unjust traditions, which should not have been started in the first place, are seemingly unyielding even as other aspects of the cultures where these traditions are carried on undergo change. The key point, which is ignored by most Western thinkers, is that even though many traditions are sources of socially unjust practices and seem to be unyielding, this should not become the basis for rejecting *all* traditions. The cultural processes that Batalla described will still be carried on, and in many instances the traditions will represent sites of resistance to the process of colonization that is one of the more dominant traditions in the industrialized West.

What is often ignored by Western theorists who think in the dichotomous categories of closed and open systems (traditional cultures being represented as examples of closed systems and the West being represented as the model of an open, progressive system) is that the many expressions of change that appear to make Western cultures so unique are still examples of traditions that are intergenerationally conserved. The industrial model of thinking that is applied to so many areas of daily life, from built environments to health care, agriculture, and education, has been conserved over many generations—and is even being extended into new areas such as genetically modified foods and even human reproduction. This complex set of traditions, which are mistakenly viewed as freeing us from the grip of traditions, can most easily be seen in the role that language plays in conserving the taken-for-granted cultural patterns underlying the West's industrial culture.

To stay with the example of Western technology, particularly its reliance on using the machine as the template for understanding a wide range of human processes and activities, we can trace back hundreds of years how the special form of the rational process associated with scientific and technological discovery was based on a metaphorical process of thinking encoded in the language. The conserving nature of language, even when used in the service of discovering new scientific understandings and technologies, can be seen in how Johannes Kepler's (1570–1630) description of the "celestial machine" (the universe and all its component parts) should be understood as a "clockwork" has been conserved and only slightly modified in terms of the scientists' ability to account for even smaller "component parts" of the life processes they still represent as a machine. While Newtonian science and the last-several-hundred-year history of medical research in the West are now being challenged, the mechanistic model of thinking is still dominant—indeed, is being extended into new areas of scientific research and industrial production. Today, leading scientists such as Francis Crick, Richard Dawkins, and E. O. Wilson use the machine metaphor to explain the most fundamental biological processes. Dawkins, for example, refers to the body as a "survival machine," while Wilson explains that "the surest way to grasp the complexity of the brain, as in any other biological system, is to think of it as an engineering problem" (1998: 102). And Francis Crick, the co-recipient of the Nobel Prize for his work on the nature of DNA, urges scientists to explain the "mechanism of such mental activities as intuition, creativity, and aesthetic pleasure" (1994: 261). It is so common today to read or hear references to how the brain is like a computer that hardly anyone notices the utter nonsense or the deeper implications of this mistaken idea—even when computer scientists are now beginning to explain how computers are about to replace humans in the Darwinian process of natural selection.

If we consider such other traditional ways of thinking in our change-obsessed culture we would find the same continuities. The tradition of thinking of the individual as the basic social unit and source of ideas and values (which ignores how language carries forward the basic conceptual patterns that the individual relies upon), that change is inherently progressive (even as we are witnessing more evidence of environmental degradation), and that cultural evolution ensures the survival of the fittest (even as we witness the global destruction of industrial approaches to food production and consumption) are examples of how the traditions underlying modern development undermine a more reflective approach to the traditions that are being undermined. That is, they represent, as in the tradition of thinking of organic processes as machinelike, the dominance of abstract and linguistically driven thinking over an awareness of ourselves as organic and cultural beings that do not fit the model of a machine. One wonders, for example, if Richard Dawkins experiences his own body as a survival machine, and if E. O. Wilson really experiences his own brain as a machine that can be re-engineered. These two examples, and there are many others that could be taken from the writings of scientists who have strayed across into scientism, indicate the problem of how the unexamined use of language can lead to the misconceptions of the past taking hold and directing current ways of thinking.

The languaging processes of a culture can also be understood as conserving the culture's approach to the built environment. In some cultures, the siting of a building must take account of the fundamental alignments that govern the universe. In effect, the nature of physical space, use of materials, accessing of light, and the human activities appropriate to different interior spaces may be dictated by the culture's mythopoetic narratives. The diverse approaches to the design and use of materials in American society can be read as message systems that convey some of the most dominant assumptions of the culture, such as individualism, level of material wealth and social status, and total indifference to fitting the design of the building to the natural characteristics of the site. In the case of vernacular architecture, the composition and design of the building may encode generations of experience of how best to utilize local materials in ways that take account of the characteristics of the local environment. For example, in the hot and humid regions of the world, it is not unusual to find the dwelling situated well above ground level, thus allowing the cooling breezes to circulate under the floor. The use of natural materials rather than sheet-metal roofs and cinder bricks, as we have learned from experience, provides for better control of interior temperatures. Even the color of buildings may reflect the accumulated wisdom of how to make the interior space of the building more comfortable—or, as is the case with the designs of an architect such as Bernard Maybeck, how to connect the interior space with the experience of the immediate outdoors. The opposite approach to the use of building materials can be seen in the glass box office buildings that require huge air-conditioning machines, and thus represent the worst in environmental design. The interior space is, in effect, insulated from the surrounding environment. Fortunately, there is an increasing awareness that buildings should incorporate elements of the local environment, such as terrace and roof gardens, and that the design and engineering process should be governed by the need to make as little disruptive environmental impact as possible. Even these ecological approaches to design must be seen as building upon the knowledge accumulated over many generations.

Any discussion of the inherently conserving nature of the cultural languaging processes needs to take account of what Samuel P. Huntington referred to as "temperamental conservatism." What he meant by this category of conservatism is that each person, regardless of culture and ideological persuasion, is comfortable with eating certain foods, manner of dress, conversations, friends, outdoor activities, and so forth. Temperamental conservatism, in effect, encompasses the taken-for-granted patterns in a person's daily life—patterns that are integral to the person's sense of identity and accustomed lifestyle. This form of conservatism has no special ideological orientation, and thus should not be judged as a distinct category of conservatism—in the way in which the word "conservatism" is used in today's political discourse. Rather the varied behavioral expressions of temperamental conservatism should be the focus of judgment, such as the person who is comfortable in exploiting others, who thinks in reactionary ways and is driven to impose his/her messianic agenda on others, who feels more alive and centered when working in the garden, who goes to the aid of others, and so forth. They are all examples of temperamental conservatism, but the way in which they are expressed is what is problematic. As many Western theorists have been educated to think of conservatism and liberalism as conceptual agendas that politicians and others use to guide their reform efforts, they too often fail to recognize the many expressions of temperamental conservatism in their own lives—even as they denounce all forms of conservatism as inhibiting the full emancipation of the individual.

Given this more culturally informed interpretation of conservatism, as well as its inescapable temperamental manifestations, the question arises as to whether the word covers so many aspects of biological and cultural life that it no longer has any explanatory power. For example, if the ideas of classical liberal thinkers such as John Locke, Adam Smith, and John Stuart Mill have been conserved by people who identify themselves as conservatives, does the word lose its ability to accurately represent a political agenda, as well as its place in the history of Western ideas? And what about the Western cultural assumptions encoded and thus conserved in the Marxists' view of the end of history? What about the temperamental conservatism of revolutionaries such as Lenin, Marx, and Mao? Or the temperamental conservatism of educational reformers who urged the continual reconstruction of experience (Dewey), the continual process of renaming the world by each individual (Freire), and the advocates of transformative learning where progress emerges out of the mix of natural selection, chaos, and the subjective constructions of supposedly autonomous individuals (a view held by the majority of teacher/educators)? It would be interesting to document the gulf that separates the temperamental conservatism of these reformers from their messianic and ethnocentric plans for rescuing what they view as the deficit cultures of the world.

Understanding the conserving nature of biological and cultural processes, as well as the conserving processes that operate at the level of personal identity and taken-for-granted practices, brings into focus that the tradition of representing liberalism and conservatism as opposing political visions of what constitutes a just society reflects a major weakness in what is being learned in Western universities. The fact that the process of conserving is what has sustained the different cultural traditions still carried forward by the nearly 6,000 languages still spoken in the world today (with many of these languages on the verge of extinction), and that the word has been grossly misrepresented by intellectuals and politicians who have been culturally and historically misinformed, does not preclude the possibility that we can begin to use it with the precision required if we are to address the cultural roots of the ecological crisis.

That is, we must begin to reclaim the deep meaning of the word if we are to take seriously the task of identifying which cultural traditions contribute to the revitalization of the commons, and which traditions were constituted on basic misunderstandings of how dependent humans are on the self-renewing capacity of natural systems. To accept the current misuse of the term by journalists, academics, politicians, and spokespersons for corporations is to surrender our critical judgment, and thus to surrender our ability to resist the globalization of the industrial culture that is undermining the diversity of the world's cultures and the viability of natural systems. As I pointed out in the early 1980s, it is futile to critique the conceptual and moral foundations of the industrial culture by relying upon the same cultural assumptions that are the basis of what is being critiqued. And as I have pointed out elsewhere, the criticism of capitalism by reformers in the Marxist tradition of thinking, such as Freire and his followers, is little more than an argument within a dysfunctional extended family. Their criticisms address real issues, but never what represents a genuine alternative to the industrial culture that is based on the same deep cultural assumptions about individualism, progress, universalizing a Western vision of a just society, authority of abstract theory and the role of the intellectual and expert, and an anthropocentric view of nature. The critics of the industrial system of production and the continuing quest for ever larger profits share with their "enemies" the same silences. Indeed, they are members of the same dysfunctional family they criticize. Their silences are becoming more recognizable as we begin to identify the characteristics of the commons, and how the diverse commons represent different cultural traditions of responding to the limits and possibilities of the local bioregions.

The challenge here is to develop further the sub-vocabulary of conservatism that will enable us to understand how educational reforms can contribute to the revitalization of the commons, and to the democratic traditions of local decision making about the renewal of intergenerational traditions that represent alternatives to the many forms of dependency that are required by the expansion of industrial culture. And in rectifying the use of conservatism, it will be necessary to clarify how conserving the nonmonetized traditions and relationships within the commons differs from the political agenda of liberalism, what is currently referred to as "free-market conservatism" that should more accurately be called faux conservatism, and libertarianism. In effect, the task is to compare the actual practices of the commons with the political agendas that are variously labeled as liberal, conservative, and libertarian. What is not being undertaken here is an examination of the various social critiques and agendas assigned to these political terms by theorists whose abstract formulations fail to take account of the diversity of the symbolic and natural systems that make up the world's commons. This task will be left up to university departments of political science. Unfortunately, this recommendation, if carried out, would likely continue the same omissions that have made so much of political theory irrelevant to addressing the cultural roots of the ecological crisis.

THE THREAT OF SOCIAL JUSTICE AND LAISSEZ-FAIRE LIBERALISM TO THE REVITALIZATION OF THE COMMONS

To reiterate a key point that needs to be kept in the forefront of the discussion of the difference between renewing the commons and the deep ideology foundations of the various interpretations of liberalism is the conserving nature of cultural and biological processes. The current view held by the proponents of these different interpretations of liberal assumptions is that what is conserved between generations is static and thus an obstacle to social progress. The recognition of the dynamic nature of cultural and biological continuities should also take account of how powerful groups may resist change—and even attempt to return to an earlier period of cultural development. A careful examination of these efforts to recover the past as a model for the present will reveal, in many instances, the use of modern technologies such as the computer which will, over time, introduce further changes in the culture's most basic beliefs and practices.

So the question is: How does a mindful conservatism approach to the revitalization of the commons differ from what appears on the surface to be four distinct political discourses that are unevenly represented in today's media and the thinking of most academics? One of the most important differences is that mindful conservatism is expressed at the grassroots level as members of a community work to renew aspects of the commons that are being threatened by both old and new forms of enclosure. The four different interpretations of how liberal assumptions are to guide social policy, the behavior and values of individuals, and relationships with other cultures and the natural environment, on the other hand, are mostly articulated by politicians, business spokespersons, and academics who rely upon abstract concepts and ideals that have been handed down over generations as guides to a better future. Unfortunately, these varied interpretations have not been revised to take account of their relevance to today's world.

Before considering the core assumptions that underlie these different interpretations of liberalism, it is important to recognize the record of achievement of social justice liberalism. Its achievements include the creation of safety nets such as social security, unemployment insurance, protection of workers' rights—as well as gains in the area of civil rights and greater equality of opportunity for minority and previously oppressed groups. In effect, the social justice tradition of liberalism has been motivated by the conviction that the instruments of government should be used to improve the lives of the more vulnerable and politically powerless segments of society. While the achievements of social justice liberals can be interpreted as contributing to the revitalization of the commons, they continue to embrace other core liberal assumptions that lead to the destruction of the commons—including the commons of other cultures. That is, the assumptions still taken for granted by social justice liberals continue to reproduce the misconceptions of the earliest founders of Western liberalism. These include John Locke's misunderstanding about the nature of language as well as his view of how private ownership of property is established, John Stuart Mill's emphasis on individual freedom and self-creation, and Herbert Spencer's evolutionary way of representing the West as more developed than non-Western cultures. According to Daniel Bell, the modern art movement further reinforced Mill's misconception that social justice liberals continue to embrace: namely, that the ideal that should guide the efforts of liberals is the self-creating individual and thus autonomous individual. This collection of liberal ideals, which differs radically from the earlier influence of the communitarian orientation of different traditions of Christianity that led to earlier liberal social justice efforts, is now framed in terms of equal opportunity for individuals to realize their personal goals in a consumer-based culture.

Educational reformers such as John Dewey, Paulo Freire, and the educational followers of Jean Piaget have further undermined the possibility that liberalism could contribute to a viable commons by making a form of critical reflection the one true approach to knowledge. And like the proponents of other interpretations of the mission of liberalism, they have given ontological status to the Western assumption about the linear nature of progress. That is, they share with the liberal proponents of globalizing the West's industrial culture (including the liberals who are wrongly labeled as free-market conservatives) the idea that critical inquiry leads to the emancipation from the hold of traditions. As Dewey put it, and as it is restated by liberal theorists who embrace the latest expression of scientism, experimental inquiry is essential to the ongoing task of reconstructing experience—a view that is also held by scientists, technology innovators, and marketing specialists who understand that the traditions of the commons must be overturned in order to create new markets. Dewey did not intend to align himself with those who promote economic and consumer growth-mania, nor was he aware that his emphasis on experimental inquiry, when imposed on other cultures as the one true approach to knowledge, contradicted his deep commitment to local democracy. As I argued in *Mindful Conservatism*, Freire's approach to critical inquiry is based on the Western liberal assumptions about progress, an anthropocentric universe, and a Social Darwinian view of stages of cultural development. The result is that his idea of emancipation simply reproduces the misconceptions that underlie the thinking of Western philosophers—a tradition of thinking that has been silent about the enclosure of the commons and the importance of cultural diversity to the preservation of biological diversity. These are silences that also characterize his writings, and those of his many followers. What these social justice liberal educational reformers ignore is that the prescriptions for what constitutes social justice cannot be imposed from outside the culture, and that its achievement must be based, as Gustavo Esteva and Madhu Suri Prakash explained (1998), on revising local norms by the members of the culture who have a knowledge of which traditions can be used to justify a more socially just community.

There are a number of fundamental differences that separate the earlier achievements of social justice liberals, as well as today's liberals who are more narrowly focused on expanding the freedom of the individual, from the mindful conservatism that strengthens the commons. At the risk of restating certain points, it is important that these differences be made as explicit as possible. The differences, or what I refer to as the limitations of liberalism, can be traced back to what the earliest liberal theorists did not understand about the world they lived in. Locke, Rousseau, Smith, and Mill, as well as the early scientists such as Bacon, Newton, and Kepler who helped to fashion a new form of consciousness that differed from the medieval state of mind, understood the individual as an autonomous social unit and source of rational thought.

This new view of the individual represented a momentous shift in Western consciousness. But it was based on a number of basic misunderstanding that are still reproduced in the thinking of liberal educational reformers who now argue that education can contribute to social progress by encouraging students to construct their own knowledge. These misunderstandings are also promoted in a variety of academic disciplines in ways that lead to the separation of knowledge into high- and low-status categories— with the high-status knowledge contributing to the further enclosure of the world's diverse commons. The key misconceptions of the early "fathers" of liberalism that are still conserved by the different interpretations of today's liberals can be summarized below.

THE LIBERAL MISCONCEPTIONS ABOUT THE NATURE OF TRADITIONS AND CULTURAL WAYS OF KNOWING

There were many cultural changes that contributed to the liberal view of the individual as an autonomous, self-directing, politically accountable agent. These include the printing press, the development of perspectivism in the arts, the rise of empiricism that located the source of the individual's ideas in direct experience, the spread of Cartesian thinking that claimed (along with Locke) that individuals are free from the influence of traditional knowledge, the rise of experimental science, and so forth. And what emerged from the convergence of these cultural changes, as well as from writings of the Enlightenment philosophers, was the idea that traditions represented the chief obstacles to progress. That is, tradition as a metaphor was associated with the vestiges of the feudal past, with the privileges and vast wealth of the church, and as the source of poverty and limited opportunity for the masses.

This narrow and essentially negative view of tradition continues today to be a central feature of liberal thinking—from the social justice liberals across the spectrum of interpretations that now includes the proponents of a society based on libertarian thinking. This critical view of tradition has made a genuine contribution when directed at such cultural practices as the exploitation of workers, the denial of civil rights and equal opportunities for minority groups, the many past and current expressions of corporate malfeasance—and to the traditions of reducing the environment to an exploitable resource. However, the liberal tradition of thinking of traditions only as sources of oppression and economic exploitation has led them to ignore the many traditions that are the basis of civil society, sources of community and individual self-reliance, and the many forms of knowledge and practices that have improved the quality of everyday life. The liberals' singular focus on the oppressive nature of traditions, combined with their support of the myth that equates new technologies (and forms of enclosure) with progress, has resulted in a widespread failure to ask what traditions are being undermined or entirely overturned by new social and mechanical technologies, by politicians seeking to serve the special interests of corporations and powerful voting blocs, by international trade agreements such as NAFTA and the WTO, and by new scientific discoveries in the area of mind-altering drugs and genetically modified seeds.

Without this more balanced understanding of traditions, which is not presented in our public schools and universities and which is further exacerbated by the formulaic thinking of many liberals who identify any expressions of concern about the loss of traditions with so-called conservatives and religious fundamentalists, today's liberals fail to ask the basic question about what is being lost as the influence of industrial culture spreads into every aspect of daily life—from the industrialization of every phase of growing and preparing food, children's toys, ways of encoding and communicating knowledge, entertainment, health care, and so forth. If the reader thinks this criticism of the liberals' failure to ask what needs to be conserved in this era of ecological uncertainty and growing dependence upon an industrial-dictated lifestyle, I suggest that he or she survey how university graduates understand the nature of tradition. From my experience of teaching at several universities and talking with students at a number of foreign universities, I found that most of students associate traditions with holidays and the celebration of special family and religious events.

A second consequence of carrying forward (conserving) the conceptual misunderstanding about the complex nature of traditions (a word that is as encompassing as the word "culture"), is that liberals are particularly insensitive to the importance of the traditions of other cultures. This insensitivity shows up in many ways. References to the traditions of self-sufficiency of many indigenous cultures are generally criticized by liberals on the grounds that "we cannot go back to a more primitive state of existence"—a response that reveals that the Social Darwinist interpretative framework is still alive and well in many liberal circles. And if this generalization is considered too unsupported by evidence I suggest that the reader check our what scientists such as Carl Sagan claim to be the difference between Western rationally based knowledge and the knowledge systems of non-Western cultures. His combination of ethnocentrism and hubris is forcefully articulated in *The Demon-Haunted World: Science as a Candle in the Dark* (1997). It is reiterated in E. O. Wilson's highly acclaimed book, *Consilience: The Unity of Knowledge* (1998), and in Francis Crick's *The Astonishing Hypothesis: The Scientific Search for the Soul* (1994). Other liberal and so-called conservative academics reinforce the misunderstanding about the importance of the community-sustaining traditions of non-Western cultures by relying upon silence to convey the message that the traditions of other cultures are not worthy of even being named. As the ability to think about the Other is dependent upon possessing the language for making explicit what is either taken for granted or what is not known, this silence is a powerful form of denial. The exceptions to this university-wide condition of liberal ethnocentrism can be found in the departments of anthropology and cultural linguistics; but even in these departments the liberal bias is widespread—and growing again as Darwin's theory of natural selection is being rediscovered as a way of explaining the more evolved nature of Western cultures.

The widespread habit of separating traditions and critical rationality into two distinct and opposing categories leads liberals into the moral quagmire of promoting development schemes that often are thinly masked efforts at economic and cultural colonization. This tradition of viewing other cultures as in a state of backwardness, as deficit cultures, provides the justification for social justice–oriented liberals to promote literacy schemes that foster a Western form of consciousness, to urge educational reforms based on Western assumptions about the importance of students learning to construct their own knowledge and identities, and to adopt computers as a means of acquiring more information that will facilitate economic development. That the traditions of the non-Western cultures might be undermined by these efforts, thus opening them to colonization, becomes a nonissue for liberals who combine their ethnocentrism with the messianic drive to convert others to the liberals' understanding of what constitutes a more socially just and progressive state of existence. The double bind that Edward Shils refers to as the "anti-tradition tradition" of most liberals shows up in their failure to recognize that many of the nonmonetized, intergenerationally based traditions of non-Western (especially indigenous) cultures provide the basis of resistance to the further enclosure of the commons—a phenomenon, as pointed out earlier, that liberals have largely ignored. Indeed, to take seriously the various forms of enclosure and cultural colonization is to think like a mindful conservative.

THE LIBERAL MISCONCEPTIONS
ABOUT THE ENVIRONMENT

Many environmentalists, in wanting to avoid identifying themselves with the agenda of the politicians and media figures such as Rush Limbaugh, consider themselves to be liberal activists. Thus, they are likely to react with surprise to my claim that they are the mindful conservatives, and that the genuine liberals who think in the tradition established by John Locke, Adam Smith, and recent liberal economists such as Milton Friedman, view the environment as an exploitable resource. If we review the early and largely unacknowledged roots of liberal thinking, from the mythopoetic narratives such as the Book of Genesis to the philosophers who promoted abstract theory over culturally grounded ways of thinking, as well as the political theorists who explained how property becomes an individual possession, we find no discussion of human/nature relationships that resembles Aldo Leopold's "Land Ethic." The history of liberal thought, as well as current liberals who are mistakenly called conservatives and who are promoting the globalization of the West's industrial and environmentally destructive culture, has equated individual and social progress with transforming the commons into the mega-shopping malls that autonomous individuals are increasingly dependent upon. The first voices in America that were raised against exploiting the environment, and that articulated the need for moral reciprocity within a broader understanding of the commons—Henry David Thoreau, John Muir, Theodore Roosevelt, Aldo Leopold, Rachel Carson—were conservationists. That is, their basic orientation was to conserve the biological diversity that all life-renewing processes depend upon.

The inability of liberals to recognize the importance of protecting the commons from further enclosure, and thus the importance of a conserving ethic, can be seen in the increasingly close integration of the culture of Western universities with the culture of the corporate world. The recent awakening of some academics to the nature of the ecological crisis has mostly taken the form of using science to promote greater efficiency in eco-management. Critics who are pointing out the many ways in which universities and public schools are complicit in promoting the cultural values and ways of thinking that underlie the global spread of the West's industrial/consumer dependent culture are still largely ignored. And educational reformers such as Moacir Gadotti and Paulo Freire, who have recently become aware of the ecological crisis, seem unable to recognize that their liberal assumptions about the need for the world's cultures to adopt the core assumptions underlying the Western pattern of thinking cannot be reconciled with the diverse cultural approaches now being taken to revitalize the commons.

It is also important to note that the so-called culture wars between liberals and faux conservatives (who should more properly be referred to as "reactionaries" because of their desire to go back to earlier traditions) have totally ignored the cultural and thus educational roots of the ecological crisis. A critique of the Western canon is still needed, especially if the critique is framed in terms of how the history of the formative thinkers in the West laid the conceptual and moral basis for equating the destruction of the world's commons with social progress, and for ignoring that the ideal of the autonomous rational individual is, over the long term, ecologically unsustainable.

LIBERAL MISCONCEPTIONS ABOUT THE NATURE OF LANGUAGE AND INDIVIDUALISM

My earlier writings on the cultural nature of intelligence led to the criticism that I am against individualism and for oppressive traditions. This response from liberal educational reformers who have made the project of ongoing emancipation (and thus individual autonomy) the primary goal of the educational process simply reflects what Gregory Bateson calls an ecology of bad ideas that are still the central dogma in most Western universities. At the core of this dogma are two misconceptions that have been buttressed by Western philosophers, by generations of university professors who reproduced (an expression of mindless conservatism) the conceptual errors of their mentors, and by a system of penalties that are imposed when the misconceptions are challenged. These misconceptions also serve as the linchpin of the different interpretations of liberalism. That is, they are basic to both social justice and to market-oriented liberals.

The long-held tradition of thinking of rational thought as an attribute of the autonomous individual, as well as viewing the individual as determining what values to live by, are both based on a misunderstanding about the role that language plays in influencing thought and the choice of values. Part of the reason for ignoring the influence of language can be traced to the way in which most of the culture that a person is born into is learned in context and at a taken-for-granted level of awareness. The tradition of liberal philosophers who emphasized that individuals could control their own destiny as they exercise rational thought further marginalized the need to be aware of the multiple ways in which thought and behavior were influenced by the culture's languaging processes. This long tradition of equating rational thought with individualism is currently being further strengthened by the widespread use of computers, and the promotional arguments that claim that access to data further empowers the rational process of the individual. The example cited earlier of how such acclaimed scientists such as E. O. Wilson, Francis Crick, and Richard Dawkins reproduce the same metaphorical language that Newton and Kepler used to represent organic processes as having the characteristics of a machine, could be extended to many other areas of culture where earlier culturally specific ways of thinking are carried forward over generations—and continue to influence the thinking of our most acclaimed scientists, philosophers, social theorists, and educational reformers.

The basic process that leads current thinkers to reproduce the conceptual patterns of earlier generations that may extend back hundreds, even thousands of years, is part of the implicit way in which the culture is learned. It is a process that takes place in all cultures, but the colonizing and environmentally destructive nature of Western culture now makes it imperative that the liberals who now have such influence in establishing what constitutes high-status knowledge must begin to recognize the dynamics of how language reproduces the misconceptions that now underlie their agenda for the rest of the world's cultures. The way in which earlier patterns of thinking are derived from the mythopoetic narratives such as those found in the Book of Genesis, and the powerful evocative experiences (thinking of living processes as machinelike and the influence of the constant stream of technological innovations that give humans greater control and ease the burden of certain aspects of work) are what has formed the basis of much of the metaphorical language used in the West. These basic cognitive schemata, or what I call root metaphors that influence the process of analogic thinking, and over time become encoded in our image words, are now the taken-for-granted basis of liberal thinking. These conceptual footings or root metaphors include individualism, a linear form of progress, mechanism, anthropocentrism, evolution, economism (that is, transforming every aspect of the commons into a commodity), and patriarchy (which is now being challenged within certain segments of society—but still held onto by reactionary groups). Each of these root metaphors contributes to shaping different areas of cultural practice, and some are now being challenged by the emergence a new root metaphor: ecology—which is the root metaphor of mindful conservatives. Indeed, this metaphor provides the basis for understanding the interdependencies within the commons, and it does so in a way that takes account of different cultural approaches to the commons that are sustainable.

The different interpretations of liberalism are dependent upon maintaining the misconception that represents language as a conduit through which autonomous individuals communicate their ideas. The myth of language as a conduit is also central to the idea that computers simply transmit, store, and manipulate "data." Indeed, even the idea of objective data is dependent upon this misconception about the nature of language. And if professors and classroom teachers understood how language encodes earlier processes of metaphorical thinking that were influenced by the culture's constitutive root metaphors, they would find it more difficult to maintain the mutually reinforcing fictions that the student should be held accountable as an autonomous thinker, that the rational process is free of being culturally influenced, and that knowledge (now data and information) is objective.

But maintaining the conduit view of language is fundamental to liberals for other reasons that relate more directly to the liberals' history of colonizing other cultures, and to the liberals' role in exacerbating the degradation of the world's natural systems. The basic misconception that represents language as a culturally neutral conduit enables the liberals to represent the key elements underlying their pattern of thinking (individualism, progress, stages of cultural evolution, a human-centered world, a conflict model of rational thought, a material view of wealth, an experimental approach to transforming cultural practices, a view of tradition as limiting progress and individual freedom, and so forth) as universals. That is, ignoring how the assumptions of their culture are encoded in the layered nature of the metaphorical language that influences their supposedly rationally determined ideas of what constitutes a progressive society enables the liberals to ignore the knowledge systems of other cultures. In addition, the key assumptions of liberals about the evolutionary nature of cultural development, as well as how the multiple ways of knowing and renewing knowledge in other cultures do not fit the liberal's emphasis on rational, critically based knowledge, and now their reliance on data and information, make it unnecessary to consider the possibility that their good intentions for transforming other cultures to their way of thinking and lifestyle are a process of colonization. Again, language plays an important role in hiding this fact. Words and phrases such as "development," "progress," "globalization," "planetary consciousness," "world community," and a "wired world," suggest a universal consensus that is in reality an expression of the liberals' ethnocentrism, messianic spirit, and desire to impose their higher truths— and for the free-market liberals and faux conservatives, to expand their control over the economies of the world.

The basic problem with liberalism as a guiding ideology is that its key assumptions cannot be reconciled with revitalizing the commons in rural and urban North America, and the even more culturally diverse approaches to the commons in other parts of the world. Even the social justice tradition of liberalism, for all of its achievements, is caught in a double bind that undermines the sense of intergenerational responsibility so essential to the commons. The genuine contributions of social justice liberalism have been achieved by using the legislative powers of the federal government to over-turn reactionary, oppressive, and exploitive traditions that seemed unyield-ing at the level of the community, factory, and educational institution. But at the same time, the values and assumptions about the nature of the autonomous individual, progress, an anthropocentic universe, and equality in a consumer-driven culture that lead to more socially just laws in the area of human rights continue to undermine the intergenerational and ecological sense of connectedness and responsibility that are essential to a sustainable commons.

In effect, the different expressions of liberalism lack an understanding how individuals are nested in their culture, and how the culture is part of and thus dependent upon the larger ecology of natural systems. The result is that the liberal emphasis on individuals creating themselves, including where they end up in the society's status systems, has led many individu-als to rely upon material achievements to communicate who they are and their level of success and importance. This, in turn, has led to a culture of supersizing of houses, SUVs, food, body size, and individual and national indebtedness—which is now in the range of a trillion and a half dollars of personal debt. This trend returns more profits for corporations, which in turn enable them to buy more politicians who will enact legislation that will put the world's commons further at risk.

THE DIFFERENCES BETWEEN MINDFUL CONSERVATISM AND THE MISNAMED FREE-MARKET "CONSERVATIVES"

The current misuse of political labels by politicians, journalists, so-called conservative talk-show hosts, and academics conveys the impression that there are clear differences between liberals and conservatives. The fact that at the level of daily experience everybody reproduces many of the taken-for-granted patterns of their culture reduces these supposed differ-ences, and brings out that the differences highlighted in the media and by talk-radio hosts are mostly at the level of abstract ideas that are to guide policy decisions. To make this point in another way, people across the political spectrum live in ways that conserve a wide range of cultural pat-terns, from the use of nonverbal patterns of communication, to viewing themselves as individuals with their own unique perspective, to basing their thinking on the deep cultural assumptions that I have cited above. This conservatism of everyday life does not mean that there are no differences in the social policies promoted by liberals and faux conservatives. However, if only the differences in how social justice issues are perceived by liberals and so-called conservatives are taken into account, the deep cultural assumptions that both groups share in common will be overlooked. And these deep assumptions influence not only what will be given attention, such as the need to alleviate poverty and discrimination for the social justice liberals and the need to eliminate government regulation of corporations for the faux conservatives; they also influence what will be ignored. For example, even the social justice liberals do not ask about what should be conserved as the so-called conservative agenda transforms more of daily life into a greater dependency upon consumerism. And ironically, these faux conservatives do not ask what traditions in the areas of civil liberties, intergenerational knowledge, cultural diversity, and in sustainable environmental practices should be conserved. There are social groups such as the Amish, Mennonites, indigenous cultural groups, immigrants, and even networks of Anglo and Euro-Americans who are clear about their identities and patterns of mutual aid and moral reciprocity within their communities. These consciously conservative groups, however, are not the ones that are being referred to in the public discourse between liberals and the faux conservatives.

The shared silence about what needs to be conserved does not trouble the faux conservatives such as President George W. Bush, Karl Rove, and Rush Limbaugh, as they think that competition and free-market capitalism are simply the cultural version of Darwinian selection. When we consider the agenda of these self-proclaimed conservatives we find that they are in the classical liberal tradition of thinking. This can be demonstrated by asking what these "free-market conservatives," as one journalist referred to them, want to conserve. Their answer, which is usually framed as the "American way," includes the following: competitive individualism, the use of government to enforce contracts but not to provide for the well-being of the individuals and social groups that lack the ability to succeed in a capitalist-dominated society, the need to ensure progress through constant technological innovation and the expansion of global markets, the need to reduce governmental regulation of corporations—particularly in the area of environmental restrictions, and the need to continually "grow" the economy.

It is interesting to note that liberals also share the idea that the well-being of society is dependent upon growing the economy. They also share with these so-called conservatives the assumption that the creation of a global monoculture is a goal that should be worked for. The liberals are more likely to justify the need to eliminate the diversity of cultures on the grounds that it will allow democracy to be practiced more widely, while the so-called conservatives will justify the need for a global culture on the grounds that it would allow corporations to expand their markets and to become more efficient producers. I suspect that readers will again think that I am overgeneralizing about the similarity of liberal and conservative thinking about the need for a global culture based on a Western way of thinking. The support for this generalization can be found in the way that John Dewey and Paulo Freire, as liberal educational reformers, urged that all the world's cultures should adopt their respective one true approach to knowledge and decision making: the method of experimental inquiry for Dewey and critical reflection for Freire. Other educational reformers are now urging that "transformative learning" should become the standard for all of the world's cultures. How the agenda of cultural hegemony comes so naturally to liberal educational reformers can be seen in Henry Giroux's recommendation that teachers in Islamic cultures should become "transformative intellectuals" (2002: 46). The liberals who are promoting the global use of computers, and even arguing that computers will replace humans in the process of evolution, are even more closely aligned with the faux conservatives who equate globalization with global markets.

The differences between mindful conservatism and the free-market conservatives, if I can use that oxymoron here, can be easily identified. To reiterate: the focus of the mindful conservative is on the revitalization of the commons that is under threat from what Herman Daly referred to as the "growthmania" of industrial culture. The issues that concern the mindful conservative include addressing the eco-justice issues that are becoming more acute as a result of the drive to bring more aspects of cultural and biological life under the control of the industrial culture, the importance of conserving the diversity of the world's cultural approaches to maintaining viable commons, the need to foster greater responsibility for renewing the intergenerational knowledge that can serve as the basis of mutual support systems and self-reliance within communities—thus reducing dependency upon consumerism to meet daily needs while conserving the gains made in the areas of civil liberties, racial and gender equality, and workers' rights.

These social justice concerns are essential to a morally coherent life within the commons, and differ from those of the liberals, who frame their social justice concerns as achieving equal opportunity within the industrial culture where the economic/political forces and technological innovations that reduce the need for workers will continually expand the number of people who are forced into poverty.

Universities have played an important role in contributing to the misuse of our basic political categories. Few university graduates understand how they conserve cultural patterns in their daily life. Nor do they understand that there is a history of Western political theorists who wrote about what they considered to be the fundamental differences between liberalism (as they understood it in their day) and conservatism. Thus, few students graduate with an understanding of the deep cultural assumptions, as well as the silences, that characterize the history of liberal thinking. And even fewer students have knowledge of the differences between conservative thinkers. Many conservative theorists held deeply problematic ideas, such as Burke's defense of the stratified society of aristocratic England and his deep distrust of direct democracy—which was also shared by American conservative thinkers such as Alexander Hamilton and Fisher Ames. Other conservative thinkers such as John Randolph and John C. Calhoun argued for state's rights—which was really an argument for protecting the tradition of slavery. Still other conservative thinkers have based their prescriptions for the correct ordering of society on the Biblical account of original sin. This view of the human condition is now a central feature of the political agenda of fundamentalist and evangelical Christians who are striving to overturn another long-standing tradition that genuine conservatives should be defending: the separation of church and state.

The general public, and university graduates in particular, need to understand these differences in conservative thinking—which is profoundly different from being indoctrinated into accepting any one of these traditions of conservative and faux conservative thinking. Knowledge of the history of Western political thought would enable people to identify the fundamental issues and concerns that different self-proclaimed conservatives stand for—and thus whether they should be supported. Many earlier conservative theorists took positions that seem irrelevant to addressing the challenges we now face, yet understanding their silences, the concerns of their day, and their prescriptions for social reform would be useful in understanding how they differ from today's mindful conservative thinkers and activists. Just as there are extrapolations of basic liberal assumptions that have led to extremes, such as an unrestrained market economy and the idea that each individual and generation must construct its own knowledge, there are expressions of conservative thinking that would set back the gains made in the areas of social justice and tolerance of cultural diversity.

There are also core conservative insights that should be considered as relevant to identifying the cultural practices and ways of thinking that are more ecologically sustainable. For example, a careful reading of Edmund Burke and such contemporary conservative thinkers as Clinton Rossiter, Robert Heilbroner, Robert Bellah, and Alasdair MacIntyre will reveal a variety of powerful insights that should be central to today's political discourse. The misuse of the word "conservative" by reactionary elements in society as well as by politicians and spokespersons for the interests of corporations has led some of these conservative thinkers to identify themselves with liberalism—and thus to accept being caught in the double bind of identifying with the Western assumptions that have contributed to the social and ecological crisis we now face. Their writings clarify why it is important to constantly re-establish the balance between the self-direction of the individual and responsibility to the community, between developing one's own talents and interests and renewing the collective heritage that will contribute to the well-being of future generations, and between knowledge gained from community-centered experience and the abstract knowledge that is so much a part of our print-based culture. Mindful conservatives ask questions that are seldom raised by liberals who are enamored by the seemingly endless potential of technology, such as Heilbroner's concern about the limits of governmental intervention in the life of the individual. At what point, he asks, does the intervention that is intended to reform or perfect the individual cross a line that violates the rights and distinctiveness of the individual? In short, "what are the limits of social reform?"—a question that is made even more relevant today by the scientific advances in developing mind-altering drugs and in the genetic engineering of organic processes.

The conservative thinkers cited above share a common set of omissions. That is, none of them address the environmental issues that are becoming increasingly important. Nor do they frame their discussion of conservatism in terms of the wide range of cultural knowledge systems—an omission that continues to be the Achilles' heel of American foreign policies. There are, however, a number of conservative thinkers who are deeply concerned about the rapid degradation of natural systems, and they must be viewed as the best examples of mindful conservatism. The names that come most easily to mind include Wendell Berry, Thomas Berry, Wes Jackson, Stephanie Mills, Jerry Mander, Helena Norberg-Hodge, David Suzuki, Susan Griffen, and Charlene Spretnak. Again the double bind comes into play as the confusion that now characterizes the popular political discourse has led many of these genuinely conservative thinkers to avoid identifying themselves as conservatives. Mindful conservative thinkers and activists who reflect a Third World perspective include Gustavo Esteva, Guillermo Bonfil Batalla, Julio Vallodolid Rivera, Grimaldo Rengifo Vasquez, Jorge Ishizawa Oba, Vandana Shiva, and Masanobu Fukuoka.

To refer to these environmental and community activists as progressive, liberal, or free-market conservatives would fundamentally misrepresent their central concerns—which include revitalizing the local traditions of community self-sufficiency that have a smaller ecological footprint. As they view the agenda of both progressive liberals and free-market conservatives as leading to the further centralization of power in the growing alliance between the state, the militarization of the economy and foreign policy, and the global reach of corporations, they must also be viewed as resisting the worldwide spread of poverty. To reiterate a key point, the revitalization of the commons is not only a form of resistance to the globalization of industrial culture, it also contributes to the revitalization of the intergenerational knowledge that empowers people within different cultures and bioregions to rely more upon their own skills and talents—rather than to become increasingly dependent upon Western consumer products that require participating in a money economy that devalues their traditional knowledge and skills.

THE DIFFERENCES BETWEEN MINDFUL CONSERVATIVE APPROACHES TO THE COMMONS AND LIBERTARIANISM

The earlier reference to libertarianism as the bridge between the current interpretations of classical liberal ideas and the free-market conservatives that are now being promoted by Congress, and by the right-wing radio talk show hosts, is supported by Richard Weaver, who was a Professor of English at the University of Chicago. In a chapter titled "Conservatism and Libertarianism," he wrote:

> The libertarian, if my impression is correct, is a person who is interested chiefly in "freedom from." He is interested in setting sharp bounds to the authority of the state or other political forms over the individual. The right of the individual to an inviolable area of freedom as large as possible, is thus his main concern. Libertarianism defined in this way is not as broad a philosophy as I conceive conservatism to be. It is narrower in purview and it is essentially negative, but this negative aspect is its very virtue. (1998: 73)

His reference to the need to radically limit the control of the state in order to maximize the freedom of the individual might, for the casual reader, suggest that the core tenet of libertarianism is also the basis for revitalizing the commons. At the same time, a superficial understanding of the commons might lead to viewing public education, the legislation that allows industries to ignore their destructive impact on the environment, and the other governmental regulations as a threat to local decision making that is one of the main characteristics of a healthy and sustainable commons. To recall, I have presented an argument in previous chapters that connects educational institutions, the economic agenda of so-called conservative politicians, and the globalization of industrial culture—and claimed that they contribute to undermining the commons.

However, as the core tenets of libertarian thinkers are considered more closely, the differences that separate the practices and ways of thinking that contribute to a sustainable commons from the libertarians' extreme interpretation of classical liberal thinking become more evident. First, the libertarian argument that the "individual has an inviolable area of freedom," as Weaver put it, is based on a view of the individual as a rational, self-directing individual. What is particularly important about their view of autonomous individuals is their assumption that the individual is not influenced by the culture he or she was born into. Murray Rothbard, who was the founder of the Libertarian Party, summarized the human qualities that are the basis of the individual's supposedly innate freedom in the following way. In reading the following quote it should be kept in mind how Rothbard, while identifying freedom as an innate quality, reproduces his culture's taken-for-granted patriarchal pattern of thinking.

> Since *men* can think, feel, evaluate, and act only as individuals, it becomes vitally necessary for each *man's* survival and prosperity that *he* be free to learn, choose, develop *his* faculties, and act upon *his* knowledge and values. This is the necessary path of human nature; to interfere with and cripple this

process by using violence goes profoundly against what is necessary by *man's* nature for this life and prosperity. Violent interference with a *man's* learning and choices is therefore profoundly "antihuman"; it violates the natural law of *man's* needs. (2004: 4, italics added)

A second key tenet of libertarian thinking is the idea that individuals have a right to own property by virtue of their intelligence and ability to physically adapt it to their own purposes. Rothbard is particularly explicit about this tenet of libertarianism:

in the country, the action of man is still everywhere present; men have culti-
vated the soil, and generations of laborers have mellowed and enriched it;
the works of man have dammed the rivers and created fertility where waters
had brought only desolation. . . . Everywhere a powerful hand is divined
which has molded matter, and an intelligent will which has adapted it . . . to
the satisfaction of the wants of this one same being. Nature has recognized
her master, and master, and man feels that he is at home in nature. Nature has
been *appropriated* by him for his use; she has become his *own*; she is his
property. This property is legitimate; it constitutes a right as sacred for man
as is the free exercise of his faculties. It is his because it has come entirely
from himself, and is in no way anything but an emanation from his being.
(2004: 10, italics in the original)

This statement is astonishing for a number of reasons, but the one that is most relevant to the issue of the commons is that Rothbard, in effect, con- siders the entire enclosure of the commons as rooted in the natural laws that govern the universe—and thus beyond question. It is also important to note that his use of the masculine pronoun to designate action, ownership, and rational thought, while the feminine pronoun is used to designate what "man" takes possession of and uses for his own ends, reflects the influence of a long-held cultural pattern of thinking that does not support the Weaver/ Rothbard way of representing freedom as an innate quality of the individ- ual. As representative of other libertarian thinking, where only minor vari- ations exist, their ideas are far more influenced by their unexamined cultural assumptions than by any laws of nature, or by a culturally tran- scendent rational process that cannot be proven.

A third tenet of libertarian thinking that is derived from the thinking of classical liberals, as well as from today's free-market conservatives, is the belief, to quote Rothbard again, that "the free-market economy, and the specialization and division of labor it implies, is by far the most productive economy known to man." He then goes on to claim that the free market is the foundation of modern civilization (2004: 13). Most libertarians agree with Rothbard's claim, which raises a problem that few libertarians have addressed: namely, how to reconcile the libertarian view of the rights of the individual and the "advances" of the free-market economy with the evidence of a degraded environment. Charles Murray, the coauthor of the *Bell Curve: Intelligence and Class Structure in American Life* (1994), which claimed that the level of intelligence of different racial groups is largely genetically determined, is one of the few libertarians who have commented on the environment. After arguing that the government has not protected the environment, he goes on to state that "strict property rights, *extended* rather than limited, offer the best hope of protecting the environment. Stewardship," he goes on to say, "is one of the things that private property owners do best" (1997: 123). And as corporations are also owners of property, he includes them as the best stewards of the land.

The one libertarian thinker who takes a radically different position is Murray Bookchin. As the author of a number of books that address the relationship between capitalism and the ecological crisis, including *Remaking Society: Pathways to a Green Future* (1980), and *The Ecology of Freedom* (1982), Bookchin separates himself, as well as what he calls social ecology, from the mainstream of libertarian thinkers. A key difference is his criticism of the profit motive that drives the industrial mode of production. He also argues that critical reflection has a key role to play in the creation of an ecologically sustainable society, and that the ancient Greek polis should be the model of what he refers to as libertarian municipalism—which is to replace the domination of the state. To actually hear him explain libertarian municipalism reminds one of the face-to-face town meetings of early New England. Bookchin's interpretation of libertarianism also differs from the mainstream libertarianism that Rothbard represents on such issues as gender equity, the elimination of all forms of social hierarchies, and the need to rescale human societies to fit more the model of the early Greek polis which allowed for direct participatory decision-making.

These are fundamental differences, yet there are aspects of Bookchin's libertarianism that are based on the same cultural assumptions and silences that characterize the mainstream libertarian thinkers who trace their intellectual roots to the ideas of Locke, Smith, and Mill. His emphasis on rationality (albeit a critical form of rationality) as the unique quality of humans that makes irrelevant such outside forces as the state and religion is also a core belief of mainstream libertarians such as Rothbard, Robert Nozick, and J. C. Lester.

In addition to the Promethean approach of libertarian thinkers, which carries with it the problem that their ideas for how to base society on individual autonomy have never been tested in the real world, there is another problem that has its roots in the personalities of the people who represent themselves as the agents of social change. Bookchin, for example, emphasizes participatory decision-making and the elimination of all social hierarchies. Yet at a dinner I shared with him, Carolyn Merchant, and Janet Biehl on the campus of Goddard College, Bookchin's style of thinking and conversation fit that of the traditional autocrat who is in the possession of the Truth. For example, when the name of Gregory Bateson came up, Bookchin terminated what could have been a useful exchange of ideas by declaring that Bateson was a fascist. The problem, which we have seen in the lives of other philosophers and social theorists, is that they are unable to live in accordance with what they think other people should base their lives upon. This problem becomes even more evident when we consider the many ways in which the lives of the libertarian theorists are dependent upon the complex ecologies of the cultural and natural systems they are born into.

In summarizing the primary differences between the daily activities that revitalize the commons and today's four interpretations of classical liberal assumptions that dominate the current popular political discourse, the following stand out as particularly important:

1. The revitalization of the commons, whether in the African-American communities in the east side of Detroit, in the rural Zapotec communities nestled in the mountains and valleys of Oaxaca, or in the varied communities in Eugene, Oregon, is part of the daily experience that relies upon the accumulated knowledge of the local bioregion—including knowledge of mistakes made in the past. The four interpretations of liberalism, including the social justice-oriented liberals, ignore the importance of intergenerational knowledge that is both a source of empowerment and a guide to avoiding past mistakes. Like the classical liberal theorists, they all emphasize the importance of the rational self-directed individual—which is variously interpreted to mean that individuals rely upon their own rationality to overturn all of the traditions handed down by previous generations, and to construct their own knowledge.

2. The on-the-ground cultural practices and ways of thinking that contribute to revitalizing the cultural and natural systems that constitute the commons are ignored by all four interpretations of today's liberal and faux conservative spokespersons. Bookchin is the lone exception, and the social ecology that he helped to articulate is still influenced by those aspects of Marxist theory that ignored that universal prescriptions cannot be reconciled with the culturally diverse and local nature of the commons. The Western myth of unending progress leads to the idea that environmental problems, if recognized, can be quickly solved through new scientific discoveries and technological innovations. The assumptions about the connections between scientific and technological advances and the linear nature of progress partly underlie the failure of liberals and faux conservatives to ask what needs to be conserved in order to ensure the prospects of future generations.

3. The ongoing task of revitalizing the commons in different regions of the world takes place within the conceptual and moral framework of local cultures, whereas the vision of the good and socially just society envisioned by all four interpretations of liberalism reproduces the combination of extreme ethnocentrism and hubris that led the early fathers of liberalism to represent their ideas as universally valid—and as a basis for judging the backwardness of other cultures. To make this point in a different way, the combination of ethnocentrism and hubris led then and leads now to a colonizing attitude toward the cultures that have developed in different ways.

The culturally diverse approaches to revitalizing the commons differ from the four interpretations of classical liberal assumptions on the fundamentally important issue of enclosure. The free-market liberals (faux conservatives) view the process of enclosure as the expression of progress. The social justice liberals, while generally critical of capitalism, are locked into a set of beliefs about the connections between individualism and social progress that prevents them from recognizing that the daily practices that renew the commons, including the intergenerational knowledge of how to live less consumer-dependent lives, is the expression of a far more important form of resistance than what has become the ritualized writings about the power of critical reflection to emancipate individuals from all traditions.

Given the renewed attention that is being given to revitalizing the commons in different regions of the world (e.g, India, Africa, the Americas,

Japan, and so forth) the question that now needs to be considered is the role that education can play in helping students understand the many forms of enclosure, and in strengthening the nonmonetized activities, relationships, and forms of knowledge within their communities. That is, what changes must take place in our approaches to education if we are to limit and, where possible, reverse our dependence on a technology/consumer driven culture that is poisoning the natural systems that all life depends upon? This is the question that will be considered next.

Chapter Six

The Choice Before Us: Educational Reforms That Revitalize or Further Enclose the Commons

The diversity of the world's cultural knowledge systems that influence whether the local commons will continue to exist on a sustainable basis is now being threatened by the youth who are turning away from the intergenerational knowledge of their communities. This is happening across rural and urban North America, as well as in many other Western and non-Western countries. It is especially important, therefore, that the influence of modern consumer-oriented values and media images on what youth should emulate needs to be in the forefront of thinking about the long-term consequences of the educational reforms that are being promoted in North America and in other parts of the world. Taking seriously the suggestion that there is one approach to educational reform that should be taken in all of the world's cultures would be to make the mistake of masking an imperialistic agenda behind the Western God-words of individual autonomy, technological progress, and democracy. These God-words, as pointed out earlier, are based on culturally specific assumptions that have not led to social policies and collective behaviors that have a smaller adverse impact on the commons. As educational reforms need to be understood within the context of each culture as it comes to terms with the need to conserve the biodiversity essential to its future generations, I will limit the discussion of educational reforms to what needs to be addressed in North America—and other regions of the world where Western assumptions and values are being aggressively promoted. The media and entertainment industry are arguably the most powerful sources of miseducation. But as the people who run the corporations that are in the business of shaping consciousness are themselves graduates of the public schools and universities, I shall further limit the discussion of educational reforms to these institutions.

The analysis of one of the most influential approaches to educational reform, which involves the increasing dependence on computer-mediated learning, also has implications for how educational reform is being promoted in non-Western cultures. If local cultures in other parts of the world have not yet been pressured to adopt this approach to educational reform they will shortly face the decision of whether to allocate their limited resources for the purchase of computers for the classroom or face again the criticism that they are culturally backward—as was the case when literacy was used as the basis for classifying cultures as either modern or premodern. The other Western approach to educational reform that is also being promoted in a number of non-Western and Third World countries, which is called "constructivist learning," will receive only a brief mention here as I have discussed in depth how it represents a form of cultural imperialism in a book titled *The False Promises of Constructivist Theories of Learning: A Global and Ecological Critique* (2005).

COMPUTER-BASED EDUCATIONAL REFORMS: HOW THE TROJAN HORSE PROMOTES THE ENCLOSURE OF THE COMMONS

In the West the computer has become one of the most ubiquitous features of formal and informal approaches to education. Regardless of whether it is a public school or university classroom, whether the class is in the liberal arts or a required class leading to one of the professions, whether it is in a charter school or a home schooling situation, whether it is an elite private school or an impoverished school where teachers and students perceive themselves as being cheated by the absence of computers, computers are now considered essential to successful learning and to future employment. Indeed, they are viewed by many educational reformers as more essential than libraries, as well as a way of compensating for the teacher's often poor grasp of factual knowledge.

Before raising questions about the optimism, silences, and general misconceptions that characterize how the educational uses of computers are understood, it is necessary to acknowledge a number of ways in which the use of computers contributes to strengthening the commons. While some individuals and organizations create web sites to spread their hate and fascist propaganda, others have used computers to share information about the nature and locations of toxic waste sites, the effects of environmental damage on the public's health, and the efforts in different parts of the world to strengthen the commons. For example, the Green Map System (greenmap.com) was started in 1995 as a way of helping communities to share knowledge of local ecosystems and cultural resources. The maps, in effect, identified the non-enclosed green spaces, environmental resources, and culturally significant sites. The idea of mapping the environmentally and culturally significant spaces is now being adopted in towns and major cities around the world. Computers now make it possible for anyone to access this information, and to add information about local green spaces to the web site.

The web site for Slow Food, which now has a worldwide membership of over 60,000 people, is another example of how the Internet can be used to strengthen the commons. The Slow Food Manifesto, which was approved in 1989 by delegates from 20 countries, represented a quiet rebellion against the growing dominance of industrially processed food. The guiding principles of the Manifesto emphasized the importance of reviving the culturally diverse approaches to food that took account of local soils, climate, traditional recipes, and the need to recover the importance of a meal shared by the entire family. In effect, the Slow Food movement represents an effort to recover the importance of intergenerational knowledge that is essential to a more healthy lifestyle, to a community of memory and ethnic identity, and to a more sustainable natural environment.

A third web site that deserves special mention as yet another example of the usefulness of computers is the Digital Library of the Commons. Unlike the two previously mentioned web sites that promote on-the-ground commons-sustaining activities, the DLC site serves as a resource for scholars interested in what has been written about various threats, debates, and research that relate to the commons. Thus, it serves as a clearinghouse that makes important contributions to strengthening the efforts to formulate public policies that protect various aspects of the commons from the economic forces that seem to grow more powerful every day.

But there is a down side to computers that goes largely unnoticed because of the tendency to emphasize only the positive side of the uses of computers. For example, computers are seen as overcoming the linear pattern of thinking that characterizes the way most books are written, as well as the dated nature of books. Computers, in effect, are widely understood as an open window onto the world of information and recorded historical events, with the only limitation being the students' inability to know which keys to press that will access information that would otherwise be unavailable to those who only have access to books, and by teachers who mostly reproduce what they have learned from their teachers (a genealogy of consciousness that is often highly problematic). In addition to these advantages, the computer is seen as allowing students to access a seemingly limitless world of visual images, historical and contemporary accounts—and to exchange over the Internet ideas and personal interests with other students. Another assumed educational advantage of the computer is that it is seen as especially accommodating of the students' current style of thinking and writing. That is, it allows for a stream-of-consciousness style of writing. After an outpouring of ideas and facts, the student can then go back and achieve a more thoughtful form of organization—and even insert quotes and material taken from other sources. Students can even go to sites where entire papers can be purchased and then represented as their own work.

While the problem of plagiarism is a growing concern for high school teachers and university professors, most of them still see more advantages than disadvantages to the increasing reliance on computer-mediated learning. Indeed, many teachers and professors now view computers as essential as the air we breathe and, on the economic level, as essential to the students' employment in the industrial culture that they represent to students as the cutting edge of progress. University administrators have been even more supportive of computer-mediated learning for students in different regions of the world. These courses were thought to be the cash cow that would make up for the heavy expenditures being made on campuses in order to continually update the electronic infrastructure required by the rapid pace of change in computer technology. It must be said, however, that the offering of online university degrees has not turned out to be the economic bonanza that was first anticipated.

Given what most educators view as the educational advantages of computer-mediated learning, I want to challenge the widely held idea that the computer is simply a culturally neutral tool by explaining the many ways that computers contribute to the enclosure of the commons—and to creating a greater dependence upon the industrial culture that is further degrading the life-sustaining capacity of natural systems and contributing to a global monoculture. However, clarifying the destructive effects of computer-mediated learning should not be interpreted as a flight into romantic thinking where computers can be made to disappear because we are now beginning to understand what is being lost that is vital to our collective future. As Jacques Ellul points out in *The Technological Society* (1964), we cannot totally eliminate our reliance upon a technology once it has become part of the society's infrastructure, just as we cannot totally eliminate our reliance on the industrial approach to production and consumption. The challenge is in reducing our reliance in those areas where the technology undermines the self-sufficiency of individuals and communities, and where it has a destructive impact on the environment. In terms of computer-mediated learning, the challenge is to switch the emphasis from learning that is based on educational software and the accessing of information to learning about the cultural mediating and thus transforming characteristics of computers. That is, the primary focus should be on learning about the appropriate and inappropriate uses of computers. To make the point more directly, young students should not be encouraged to use the computer until they have acquired the conceptual basis for understanding how the culture transforming effects of computers contribute to the overwhelming of the commons by market forces. This would mean that computers should not be introduced until students are well along in the educational process; that is, far enough along to be able to make informed judgments that represent the early stages of democratizing decisions about the introduction and uses of various technologies—including computers. Introducing computers in the early grades, and even their use in graduate school when students have not acquired the conceptual basis for understanding the cultural mediating characteristics of computers, simply reinforces the long-held misconception that computers, like other technologies, are simply a tool—and whether they are used for destructive or constructive purposes depends on the values of the person or institution that uses it.

The idea that computers are simply a tool is reinforced by the idea that it is based, like other language systems, on a sender/receiver form of communication. That is, the users send their ideas, data, or questions via the computer to others, and they can access documents, information, images, and whatever else others have written or produced—and that can be digitized. The computer, as a technology that stores, categorizes, models, transmits visual images, and sends commands to other technologies, is considered as culturally neutral. As an early television commercial put it, a Buddhist in Tibet, a Greek fisherman, and a vendor in Iran can rely upon computers not to undermine their taken-for-granted cultural traditions. This way of representing the computer as a neutral technology reinforces the idea that everybody, regardless of cultural differences, gains from using the computer. As I pointed out in *Let Them Eat Data* (2000), this view of computers is yet another expression of Western colonization that is promoted by so-called experts in the computer industry who themselves lack the conceptual background necessary for understanding how computers privilege the forms of knowledge that are the basis of the West's industrial culture. For example, few if any of these computer experts understand the basic differences between a predominately print and an orally based culture—and thus how computers reinforce the decontextualized patterns of thinking associated with literacy in the West.

A brief summary of why the computer should not be regarded as a culturally neutral technology will help clarify its connections with the form of consciousness that equates progress with expanding the hegemony of industrial culture. The degree to which print-based thought and communication has been shaped by previously held Western assumptions or are the source of these assumptions is debatable. What is not debatable is that computers perpetuate the way print-based communication reinforces a taken-for-granted attitude toward the authority of knowledge that has been abstracted from its cultural context, the assumption that the various expressions of rational thought are the activities of an autonomous individual, and that change is both linear and progressive in nature. And just as most printed texts convey the false impression that the ideas and descriptions are objectively presented, the computer makes it even more difficult to recognize that what appears on the screen has a human authorship. Theodore Roszak explained the relationship between the person using the computer and what appears on the screen as "mind meeting mind." That is, the mind of the user is encountering the mind (and cultural orientation) of the people who wrote the software program, the documents, descriptions, and everything else that appears on the screen.

Few teachers, for example, are aware of this basic mind-meeting-mind relationship, which becomes a genuine problem when their taken-for-granted cultural assumptions correspond with the assumptions of the people who create the software programs—such as *The Oregon Trail* and *Sim Earth*. In addition to the other cultural assumptions reinforced in these two programs that supposedly foster the students' powers of problem solving, the students are reinforced for adopting the mindset of the European immigrants as they travel across the Oregon Trail in their quest for land that was already occupied by indigenous cultures. Sim Earth reinforces the mindset of the scientists who experiment with the genetic basis of life in the quest to create more rationally controlled ecosystems—along with the assumption of an human-centered world, that scientists are our most reliable guides to a sustainable future, and that the scientists' ability to eco-manage the environment will make it unnecessary to consider the cultural roots of the ecological crisis. The combination of entertainment with problem solving does engage the students' interests, and is thus seen by teachers as taking more of the burden off their shoulders. Similarly, it appears that students are more in control of their own education when they are encouraged to use the computer to access the seemingly limitless sources of information, and to make decisions about what is relevant to their learning project. But the same relationship continues to exist where the mind of the student is meeting the minds hidden by the mediating characteristics of the computer.

There are, in addition, two deeper and more troubling reasons that few teachers are aware of the cultural mediating characteristics of computers. The first has to do with the conviction among most teachers that computer-mediated learning prepares students to rise higher in the hierarchy of an information-based economy. That there is no real evidence that computers enhance the student's mastery of knowledge, except for minor gains in the acquiring of math skills, has not deterred most teachers from this conviction. Nor has this near-religious belief been shaken by an awareness on the teachers' part that the industrial culture that is now so dependent upon computers has moved to a stage of automation and outsourcing where fewer workers will be needed.

While introducing computers in the early grades and making them an absolute requirement for university students creates a greater sense of dependency upon computers, few teachers and professors are aware of the different ways in which computers contribute to the process of enclosure—which leads to the double bind mentioned earlier where the expansion of the industrial culture requires participating in a money economy that is undermined by the increasing level of unemployment. Ironically, (perhaps, "tragically" would be the better term here) the forms of knowledge and relationships that are the basis of a viable commons, and thus reduce the need to rely upon a regular paycheck to cover the cost of the most basic human needs, cannot be digitized without being transformed into a commodity.

The commons depends upon knowledge of the local environment, including a knowledge of environmental changes that may occur on an infrequent basis, such as the hundred-year flooding of local streams and rivers. This knowledge also includes an awareness of the different types of soil, as well as the kinds of habitats needed by the different plants and animals that are part of the bioregion. Depending upon the commons, this may require knowing the mix of predator animals that keep the various populations in check, and the conditions necessary for fish to reproduce themselves. Among the Quechua, for example, every aspect of the local environment is understood as communicating about present and future conditions. Even in what remains of the commons in North America, there is local knowledge of the cycles of natural systems. The point here is that computer-mediated learning involves, for the most part, learning about events, documents, ideas, systems, and so on that are far removed from the commons that are part of the students' embodied experience. As Gustavo Esteva points out, education should enable the youth that inhabit the cultural and environmental commons of the Zapotec to know about the local sources of water, regional mountains, wildlife, soils, et cetera rather than learning about the geography and plant and animal life in a distant part of the world. This view does not mean that learning about the environmental and cultural commons in other parts of the world is not important. Rather, it is that the knowledge of the local commons is largely excluded from the computer-mediated curriculum, just as it is excluded from a textbook-based curriculum. This criticism applies not just to the computer-distorted priorities in indigenous classrooms, but to classrooms in both rural and urban schools across the United States.

Environmental education teachers will challenge this generalization since they view computers as a powerful tool for modeling the characteristics of local ecosystems. While the use of computers in an environmental education class comes closest to providing local knowledge, the use of computers also reinforces a number of cultural assumptions that are reflected in their scientific management approach to natural systems— which is now being exploited as a market for the sale of an increasing number of technologies that measure changes in natural systems. But in the other areas of the curriculum students will be reinforced for accepting abstract knowledge as more important than what is local and context specific. As mentioned earlier, if the students are not given the vocabulary that enables them to name (that is, to make explicit) the characteristics, events, participants, and their interdependencies within their local commons, their thoughts and behaviors will be more influenced by the abstract knowledge they acquire in the classroom. One has only to consider how university students continue to think within the abstract language/knowledge systems of European theorists, even as the commons they are tacitly dependent upon undergo fundamental changes that will alter their future prospects. To sum up, computers enable the student to connect with distant cultures and environments, but they reproduce the long-held bias perpetuated by Western universities that local knowledge, especially face-to-face knowledge, has only marginal significance—except as an object of faculty research and publication.

The way in which computers contribute to the process of enclosure can more easily be understood by comparing the characteristics of largely oral and thus intergenerationally connected cultures with cultures where the growing and preparation of food, participation in entertainment, education, healing, outdoor activities, built environments, and so forth, are dictated by the logic of industrial culture. As pointed out earlier, the belief systems and practices vary widely between cultures, but there are certain shared characteristics of the cultures that are more centered on the renewal of their commons—and these are the aspects of culture that cannot be digitized. These include the ceremonies and narratives that intergenerationally renew the moral norms that govern human relationships and relations with natural systems. These are complex mind-embodied aesthetic-participatory experiences. When they are described in print or digitized they are fundamentally transformed into something that is abstract and lifeless.

In addition, learning to tell stories and to be an active participant in a social event, playing an instrument that is an important part of a ceremony, learning how to use the medicinal properties of plants, growing and preparing food, contributing to the arts of the community, and knowing how to utilize local materials that take account of weather patterns are all learned through mentoring. It would not be incorrect to say that mentoring is one of the chief approaches to intergenerational renewal of the cultural commons. In addition to the problem of transforming these living experiences into something that is abstract, and thus an object of observation by others, there is another reason that computers cannot encode these aspects of the living commons. That is, most of these cultural patterns are experienced at a taken-for-granted level of awareness and thus go unnoticed by individuals who have been indoctrinated with the idea that only explicit forms of knowledge are important. Few university professors, for example, were aware of their patriarchal patterns of thinking until feminists pointed them out—and forced them to change by getting legislation passed that provided redress from the traditions that went unrecognized by this supposedly most rational and progressive segment of society. And even fewer writers of educational software are aware of the assumptions they share with others in the dominant culture, such as viewing the environment as an economic resource and as a problem requiring better scientific management.

By marginalizing and, in many instances, replacing local, face-to-face traditions with the abstract knowledge of a print-based culture, the computer is contributing to the process of enclosure that goes far beyond the enclosure (monetization) of thinking and communication. To assess the accuracy of this generalization, students who have spent their years in classrooms where computers are heavily relied upon should be asked to name the mentors in their local communities, as well as about the range of skills and talents that these mentors nurture. They should also be asked to identify the different nonmonetized activities and traditions in their communities. Their silence, even about which traditions strengthen the community and have a smaller adverse impact on the environment, will support the point I am making about the many ways in which computers contribute to the enclosure of the commons.

There are other ways in which computer-mediated thinking and communication transform ways of thinking that over generations have been attuned to the characteristics of the local commons. So far the focus here has been on what cannot be digitized and on the way abstract knowledge is privileged over face-to-face, context-specific knowledge. But now we need to focus on how using a computer transforms the taken-for-granted patterns of thinking—even for cultural groups that are able to use software programs written in their own language. *The Homeless Mind: Modernization and Consciousness* (1974), written by Peter Berger, Brigitte Berger, and Hansfried Kellner, provides a description of the pattern of consciousness that the user of a computer is socialized to adopt—and over time takes on as taken-for-granted way of thinking. Their basic argument is that people who have interacted over generations with Western technology have adopted a form of consciousness that has been influenced by the nature of mechanical processes they interact with. And as computers are also machines that operate in terms of rules of thinking and machine-prescribed procedures, they continue to carry forward this technological form of consciousness that goes beyond what was discussed earlier about the problem of not being able to digitize taken-for-granted local knowl-

edge and face-to-face communication. Computers reproduce the conceptual patterns that are reinforced in the use of other technologies: that is,
they require a procedural and problem-solving pattern of thinking. This
way of thinking is highly useful in certain contexts, but it can also become
a barrier to participating in a mentoring relationship, developing aesthetic
talents, and to interpersonal relationships that are nonutilitarian in nature.

Other cultural assumptions and values that are also reinforced through
the use of the computer do not directly relate to its actual use. These habits
of mind include the idea that increased efficiency (which in itself becomes
a value) and profitability follow from understanding actions and life
processes in terms of their component parts, and from the scientific efforts
to study how to make the component parts work more effectively. This, in
turn, leads to thinking of measurability as the way of determining success,
and that it is natural to always be working to improve the efficiency of the
"mechanisms" of life forming and sustaining processes. The authors of *The
Homeless Mind* also identify another characteristic of consciousness that
has been influenced by the dominant place that mechanical technologies
have had in the lives of Westerners. The industrial-influenced consciousness, they argue, accepts individual anonymity as normal; that is, the personalities of the people who created the machine (including computers) and
operate it are incidental to the workings of the machine. Thus, individuals,
like the component parts of the machine, are perceived as interchangeable
(23–40). That print plays such a central role in the use of computers adds to
the experience of being an autonomous individual—making decisions
about what to access, what message to send, when to turn off the computer,
and the embodied experience of being generally physically isolated from
others (even when communicating with people halfway around the world).
Indeed, when so much information is available to individuals, why should
they seek out the elders and mentors in their community whose stories and
craft knowledge are made to seem so out of date?

When the cultural patterns of thinking that are amplified through the use
of computers are compared with the cultural patterns of thinking of the
diverse cultural approaches to sustaining the commons, we can more easily see that computers reinforce the same patterns that are basic to the
industrial culture that can only expand as it undermines the nonmonetized
traditions of the commons. Computers are highly useful in many areas of
life—in medicine, in helping to plan and operate complex systems such as
airline schedules, data collection, in various areas of research, and so

forth. But they are also responsible for improving the ability of governments to violate the civil liberties of their citizens, and for the gains in automation and the ability of corporations to outsource their manufacturing facilities—thus leading to the loss of employment. Assessing the gains and losses also needs to take account of how computer-mediated learning contributes to alienating students from the intergenerationally based processes of renewing the commons.

There is yet another aspect of computers that now needs to be considered: namely, the recent legislation (the 1998 Digital Millennium Copyright Act) that now covers anything that can be accessed on the Internet. Before the enactment of this law, the Internet was a new form of the cultural commons where ideas, works of art, information, and everything else—both significant and insignificant—was freely available to those who had the resources to keep up the with latest developments in computer technology. With the passage of this legislation, everything on the Internet has now been monetized and categorized as the private property of an individual or corporation. Downloading or using material taken from the Internet can thus become the source of a lawsuit if the person or corporation that originated the material wants to claim that their intellectual property is being stolen.

HOW CONSTRUCTIVIST THEORIES OF LEARNING CONTRIBUTE TO THE ENCLOSURE OF THE COMMONS

Among the modern industrialized forces that are undermining the commons in different regions of the world is the effort to base educational reform on what is called a "constructivist" theory of learning. This approach is increasingly being referred to as "transformative learning." The word "transformative" highlights the assumption of these reformers that learning should foster constant change—which is also what the industrial culture fosters. The different interpretations of constructivist learning have their roots in the ideas of Dewey, Piaget, Freire, and the more romantic followers of America's earlier child-centered phase of the progressive education movement. Dewey emphasized that the conceptual and moral basis of experience should be continually reconstructed by relying upon the method of experimental inquiry, while Freire urged each generation to rely upon critical reflection as the basis for renaming the world of the previous generations. While both Dewey and Freire, like other ethnocentric advocates of universal and continuous revolution, were deeply committed to addressing social justice issues, Piaget based his arguments for achieving individual autonomy on the unproven assumption that the stages of cognitive development are genetically determined. In light of my previous book (2005) that examines how the promotion of constructivist-based educational reforms represents yet another expression of Western colonization, I will summarize how constructivism is being used to support the argument that computers enhance the students' ability to learn. This will again highlight how the God-words of Western liberalism contribute to the form of individualism that is required by the industrial system of production and consumption.

As mentioned in an earlier chapter, the assumption shared by the fathers of constructivist learning theories is that the process of education should provide the students with the means of freeing themselves from the hold of traditions. That is, the goal of constructivist-based learning is to achieve the greatest degree of individual autonomy. Dewey and Freire emphasized more the importance of participatory decision-making in the ongoing task of reconstructing the traditions of previous generations. But participatory decision-making was to be based either on the use of experimental inquiry (Dewey) or critical reflection (Freire)—with all other cultural approaches to knowledge being excluded. Unlike the followers of Piaget and the romantic phase of the earlier progressive education movement, both Dewey and Freire (as well as their many followers) viewed the overturning of traditions as essential to achieving social justice in the world. The earlier reference to Gadotti's argument that an eco-pedagogy should be based "on the grand journey of each individual into his interior universe," which he envisions as leading to a "planetary citizenship," is yet another example of how the cultural assumptions underlying constructivist theories of learning undermine the ability to recognize that the more ecologically centered culture are not based on individuals constructing their knowledge—and not even on each generation replacing in Freirean fashion the knowledge of previous generations. What is common to all of the constructivist learning theorists is their imperialistic way of thinking that, if adopted by non-Western cultures, would undermine the intergenerational knowledge that is the base of local economies that limit the spread of industrial market forces.

The different interpretations of how the constructivist-based approaches to learning contribute to the promotion of computers in the classroom, and to the enclosure of the commons, can be summarized in the following way:

1. Constructivist theories of learning emphasize the immediate experience of the student, just as the use of a computer creates the false
   impression that computer-based communication and learning is unaf-
   fected by the intergenerational knowledge of the culture. What can only
   be called ignorance perpetuated by Western educational institutions of
   how we reenact at a taken-for-granted level of awareness the traditions
   of our culture leads educators to interpret the students as constructing
   their own knowledge as they sit in front of a computer, gathering data,
   accessing various forms of information, communicating with others.
   Computers are thus seen as providing more and quicker access to information that, in turn, supposedly facilitates the students' construction of
   knowledge. In addition, the use of the computer reinforces the widely
   held cultural myth, again renewed in each new generation of students
   who are processed through Western educational systems, that the use of
   language involves a sender/receiver relationship. This myth is essential
   to several other myths such as the one that holds that there is such a
   thing as objective knowledge (that is, knowledge that has no human
   authorship and has not been influenced by the cultural conceptual categories), as well as the myth that the rational process is free of any
   cultural influence. With regard to this latter myth, it would seem self-
   evident that the expression of rational thought is dependent upon the
   use of a culturally specific language that carries forward the assumptions that will illuminate, hide, and provide the way of understanding
   relationships shared by other members of the culture. But what should
   be self-evident, such as the recognition of the influence of language on
   what we think and how we understand relationships, has escaped the
   attention of most Western philosophers—as well as the constructivist
   thinkers who are promoting the idea of the rationally autonomous individual. That the educators who are promoting computer-mediated learning also ignore what should be so obvious about the metaphorical,
   thought-influencing nature of language leads to the continued dumbing-
   down of the next generation—again, in the name of progress and fuller
   participation in the Information Age.
2. The view of traditions as the source of oppression or as irrelevant to the
   subjective experience of the student, combined with the way computers
   reinforce an individual perspective on traditions as something in the
   past (that is, as an onlooker rather than as a re-enactor of traditions),
   undermines the students' ability to be mentored and, in turn, to mentor

the younger generation in the skills and talents that enrich the cultural commons. In effect, the mindset reinforced by computers, and by being reinforced by teachers for constructing their own knowledge, contributes to making mentors irrelevant. There is one exception, and that is that consumer-dependent individuals will mentor the next generation of consumer-dependent individuals. The consequences, which include the further degradation of the environment, also must be understood as further undermining what remains of the cultural commons.

3. Both constructivism and computer-mediated learning contribute to the liberal/scientific/technological project of creating a secular way of understanding human/nature relationships and the source of values. This secular way of thinking leads to an instrumental and self-interest approach to moral reciprocity. Increasingly, this secular way of thinking is being buttressed by the re-emergence of the Social Darwinism of the late nineteenth century. Today, however, the phrase "survival of the fittest" is being replaced by "Darwinian fitness," "better adapted," and "natural selection." The metanarrative, that is, the story of evolution that supposedly explains everything—including cultural developments—is also the basis of the theories of Dewey, Freire, and Piaget. Computer-based futurist thinkers such as Hans Moravec, Ray Kurzweil, and Gregory Stock rely upon the theory of natural selection to explain how and when computers are going to replace humans. And the proponents of the Western model of economic development, as can be seen in the policies of the World Trade Organization, also rely upon the theory of natural selection to justify why transnational corporations should be allowed to eliminate the small-scale producers that characterize the local economies essential to the life of the commons.

Many of the world's cultures are based on mythopoetic narratives (religious cosmologies) that provide the basis of an environmental ethic. The conferences on Religions of the World and Ecology held at Harvard University between 1996 and 1998, as well as the series of books that came out of the conferences, provide an understanding of how these mythopoetic narratives influence the environmental practices of the diverse commons of the world—and in some instances represent what is being undermined and distorted by the secularizing influence of the West's industrial culture. In the case of the mythopoetic narrative in the Book of Genesis, the representation of man as superior to all other forms of life became the basis of an ethic of appropriation and economic exploitation which has supported the unrestrained expansion of industrial culture. The key point here is that the mythopoetic narratives that are the basis of the culturally diverse ways of understanding the moral reciprocity that sustains the commons are passed along through the oral traditions of the culture. They are not constituted by supposedly autonomous individuals, nor are they maintained as living traditions when reduced to the printed word that appears on the screen of a computer. In short, both constructivist and computer-mediated approaches to learning reinforce the form of individualism that is easily manipulated by the media, and by the individual's dependence upon the market to meet daily needs that otherwise could have been partly met through mentoring relationships and the mutual support systems that accompany the intergenerational knowledge of how to live less consumer-dependent lives.

EDUCATIONAL REFORMS THAT CONTRIBUTE TO THE WORLD'S DIVERSE COMMONS

The ways in which public schools reinforce an individually and hedonistically oriented lifestyle, where the primary goal is to achieve individual success and happiness, is very much influenced by the education teachers receive as part of their university education. Thus, if significant reforms are to be undertaken in the public schools that contribute to a better balance between market forces and a viable commons, it is essential that the reforms must begin within universities. Some headway is already being made in the "greening" of university physical facilities; but this is the easy and less significant part of the reform effort. University administrators understand the importance of budgetary savings that result from designing new and retrofitting older building with more energy-efficient technologies. What is more important is that few administrators are encouraging faculty outside of the sciences to rethink the content of their courses and the focus of their research in light of global warming and life-diminishing changes occurring in other natural systems.

Recommending basic reforms of what is learned in university classes is an especially daunting challenge for a number of reasons. The continual search for the new theory or explanatory framework that will sweep through the discipline, and the drive to be at the cutting edge before it is exposed by younger academics as yet another intellectual fad, is just one of the reasons that most professors continue to be in denial about the nature of the ecological crisis. Being part of a tradition that emphasizes the importance of rational thought and theory-based explanations of historical events, and what is currently occurring in society, also contributes to a basic conceptual and moral separation between the life-supporting characteristics of the commons that they take for granted and their scholarly focus. The reward system within universities is geared toward achievements in the area of scholarship. And the scholarship, for most faculty, is largely based on the cultural assumptions that were handed down by their professors—who, in turn, reproduced the assumptions of their professors.

This observation may appear to be unwarranted by most professors. Thus, it is important to cite examples of the cultural assumptions that most of today's professors pass on to their students (including the next generation of professors) of what they learned from their own professors. These assumptions include an anthropocentric understanding of human/nature relationships, that the individual is the basic social unit and (if properly educated) source of rational thought, that change is both progressive and linear in nature, that organic processes can be described using a mechanistic vocabulary, and, until recently, that women lacked the ability to be mathematicians, scientists, historians, and so forth. Each discipline, in effect, is based on this process of reproducing with only minor variation the dominant assumptions of the previous generations of professors. In economics, it is the law of supply and demand that is independent of differences in cultural ways of knowing and values; in psychology, it may be a Freudian, behaviorist, or cognitive science conceptual framework—but what is common is that they all focus on processes occurring within the individual, and they all ignore the influence of culture. Philosophy has its own conceptual traditions, but the one that remains constant from Plato to the present is the ethnocentrism that is responsible for the intergenerationally shared silences about non-Western cultural ways of knowing—and how many of these knowledge systems take account of the sustaining capacity of the bioregion.

If we keep in mind how the languaging processes reproduce, with only minor variation, the cultural assumptions of earlier generations (even among university professors), we can more easily focus on the silences and misconceptions that contribute to undermining what remains of the commons. As the silences and misconceptions are so critical to understanding the difficulty in introducing fundamental reforms in university classes that support the commons rather than the industrial culture, it is necessary to reiterate their connections with the assumptions of the liberalism that most university faculty take for granted. The liberal emphasis on the progressive nature of competition in the market place, which professors translate as the progressive nature of competition between evidence, ideas, research findings, and discourses, marginalizes the awareness of the embodied nature of our many forms of interdependence within the cultural and natural commons.

Few students will hear their professors speak about the patterns of cooperation, moral reciprocity, and responsibilities for ensuring that the quality of life of future generations is not diminished—all important silences that undermine the prospects of the commons. The liberal emphasis on basing individual actions on critical rationality and the constant need to discover new ideas and technologies has led, in turn, to a widespread indifference to the traditions that are the basis of our civil liberties and that represent the gains in reducing the worst forms of human exploitation. As pointed out earlier, most students graduate from universities thinking of traditions as constraints on progress and individual self-expression and, in the best sense, as holidays and family gatherings.

In effect, the liberal assumptions that most university professors take for granted, and that they share with the industrial culture they criticize without recognizing their own complicity, has led to the widespread habit of misusing our basic political vocabulary. Journalists and political pundits reproduce the conceptual errors and silences of their professors, as well as the segment of the general public that has graduated from universities, by continuing to identify as conservatives the politicians and the heads of corporations that promote the globalization of the industrial system that is accelerating the degradation of the cultural and natural commons. They also identify as conservatives the religious fundamentalists that want to overturn the tradition of separation of church and state, and to replace a pluralistic society with a monoculture that fits their understanding of the word of God—which has been reinterpreted many times by the men and committees that have brought their own cultural ways of knowing to their translations of the Bible. Identifying as a conservative a president who rejects the traditions of international law, Constitutional guarantees such as freedom from unlawful restraint, and who creates a massive national debt that makes our future dependent upon the goodwill of foreign countries that are underwriting our ideologically driven policies, is yet another example of a major failure of universities.

Even the faculty that is addressing environmental and social justice issues contribute to the misuse of our political vocabulary. The widespread misconception that corporations and the politicians who use the government to advance their special interests are examples of conservative thinking has led environmentally oriented professors, as well as others concerned with reversing the degradation of the cultural and natural commons, to identify themselves as liberals. Leading newspapers thus refer to Vice President Dick Cheney as a conservative, and the environmentalists trying to stop the so-called conservatives in Congress from reversing the environmental legislation of the last 30 years as liberals. Think-tanks such as the Cato Institute and the American Enterprise Institute correctly label themselves as having a liberal agenda that promotes the free enterprise system, a survival of the fittest form of individualism, and a strong national defense that provides employment at the local level and that is best achieved by adopting a preemptive stance toward other nations that stand in the way of achieving foreign policy objectives that reflect the interests of special groups. But the formulaic thinking that is based on past misconceptions and misuse of our political vocabulary goes largely unchallenged.

What is relevant to my criticism of the conceptual failure endemic in our universities is that professors have not challenged how our political vocabulary is being misused in the media, the press, and in everyday conversations. Indeed, they continue to identify with liberalism and to remain silent about the fact that protecting the environment from further industrial exploitation, the gains made in the labor movement and civil rights, the linguistic/cultural diversity that is essential to the survival of biological diversity, the intergenerational knowledge that represents alternatives to a consumer-dependent existence, and the protecting the Constitution from the fascist tendencies now appearing in our society are the responsibilities of conservatives—that is, of mindful conservatives.

If university professors were concerned with the silences and misconceptions that now are the dominant feature of our national and massively dysfunctional political discourse, they would be attempting to extricate themselves from the double bind that their formulaic political vocabulary puts them in. And the way to do this would be to introduce students to such formative philosophical conservative thinkers as Edmund Burke, the authors of *The Federalist Papers*, T. S. Eliot, Clinton Rossiter, Michael Oakshott—as well as environmental thinkers such as Wendell Berry, Gary Snyder, Masanobu Fukuoka, and Vandana Shiva. The nonideological nature of conservatism can be understood by examining more ecologically centered cultures, as well as how becoming a member of a language community represents the deepest and often the most unyielding form of mindless conservatism. The origins of modern liberalism should also be part of the students' education, including the contribution that the early liberal thinkers made to overcoming the forms of domination that characterized the feudal social systems. The silences and misconceptions of these early liberal theorists, and how they are being reproduced by current market and even most social justice liberals should also be given attention. If professors were to become more aware of the misuse and limitations of our binary political language, they might recognize that the two terms, liberalism and conservatism, are inadequate for accurately representing the agendas of various groups. Terms such as traditionalist (those who wrongly think that traditions do not and should not change), reactionary, extremist, and fascist better describe the actions and intent of different social groups in America. And instead of referring to various religious groups that want to make the present fit their interpretation of how they are to carry out the will of God as social conservatives, it would be more accurate to identify them as Baptist conservatives, Orthodox Jewish conservatives, Moral Majority conservatives, and so forth. The political label should provide the information for the larger public to know about the group's basic beliefs and missionary agenda—and thus to have some understanding of the social changes they are attempting to bring about.

UNIVERSITY REFORMS THAT ADDRESS THE NEED FOR A SUSTAINABLE COMMONS

The role that professors can play in helping to rectify the misuse of language in our national political discourse is just one of the areas of reform that need to be given attention. Other areas of reform include addressing the misconceptions that I earlier identified with past and current liberal thinking. It is important to note, however, that unless the misuse of our political language is rectified first these other silences and misconceptions will go unnoticed—and thus will continue to contribute to our growing pariah status within the world community. At the risk of appearing repetitious, the connections between current liberal misconceptions promoted by many professors and the further enclosure of the commons need to be spelled out more fully. The DNA of liberal thinking (both in the university classroom and in corporate boardrooms) is that change is the dominant reality—and that the continual quest for new ideas is necessary for ensuring that change is progressive in nature. This formulaic thinking marginalizes, as I pointed out earlier, the need to understand the complexity of the traditions we depend upon in daily life, and use as the basis for developing new and hopefully more ecologically friendly technologies, and advances in further securing a democratic and socially just society. More importantly, it marginalizes the importance of being aware of the traditions that represent important gains in civic life, labor relationships, and being less dependent upon consumerism.

Historically, liberalism has provided the conceptual and moral legitimacy for enclosing the commons of different cultures and bioregions—in the name of literacy, economic development, and the expansion of human rights (that is, our version of human rights). The problem is that engaging in the renewal of the commons on a daily basis, as well as the political task of challenging the liberal economic forces that want to further exploit the commons in the name of progress, requires the use of a language that represents traditions as more complex than as expressions of backwardness and unenlightenment. The need to have a more complex understanding of tradition and the ability to identify the still viable and even essential traditions from those that were wrongly constituted in the first place or change too slowly, is that all the nonmonetized aspects of both the cultural and natural commons are examples of traditions that have been passed along over four generations—the amount of time that it takes for an innovation or refinement of an older tradition to become part of people's taken-for-granted world.

The growing and preparation of food, the manner of greeting a guest, the use of medicinal plants, the ability to incorporate the knowledge of local ecosystems into the design and placement of a building, the knowledge of the cycles of plant and animal life in the bioregion, and so forth, are all dependent upon traditional knowledge being passed along—and modified over the generations. These examples, from the perspective of university professors concerned with keeping current with the writings of the French theorist of the month, or advancing an already failed theory of everything—such as the current effort to use evolutionary theory to explain the genetic basis for computers replacing humans and why scientists are to be nature's agents for determining which cultures are to survive, appear too mundane and thus totally inappropriate for inclusion in a university class.

It is important to understand that the silences and misconceptions being pointed out here do not mean that professors ignore traditions entirely. The problem is that while the liberal orientation of professors leads them to continually focus on the traditions that need to be overturned, including the traditions within each discipline that young turk professors view as opportunities to advance their own careers (and often important for non-career reasons), what gets marginalized is a discussion of the traditions that need to be conserved—particularly the traditions that contribute to a lifestyle that has a smaller ecological footprint. If such discussions in class were to occur, and come to the attention of colleagues, there is the danger of being labeled as a conservative—which is, in many departments, to be identified as a pariah. There is another relationship that all professors have with the traditions of their culture. The symbolic and material aspects of the culture they rely upon to do the most basic daily tasks and to function in the office, classroom, cyberspace, and the lab, are all examples of traditions—which most professors largely take for granted. That is, traditions such as speaking in a subject-verb-object pattern, writing from left to right, using spelling and punctuation that go back to the transition from oral to print-based communication, use of metacommunication patterns, all the traditions that are the basis of current technologies, and so forth, are re-enacted without actually being acknowledged as examples of traditions that are sources of empowerment as well as sources of constraint. In making the case that a more reflective approach should be taken in the classroom and in scholarly writings to the complex nature of tradition, it thus should be kept in mind that I am arguing for educational reforms that contribute to the students' communicative competence in identifying the traditions that contribute to the viability of the local commons, and to democratizing decisions about the introduction of new economically and technologically based forms of enclosure.

There is another characteristic shared by most university professors that serves as an obstacle to understanding the diversity of the world's commons: namely, the ethnocentrism that is so widespread across departments. As few professors in political science, economics, philosophy, psychology, history, the sciences, and the professional schools have themselves studied other cultural ways of knowing, they advance the knowledge in their respective fields in ways that perpetuate the cultural assumptions that have been handed down for hundreds—even thousands—of years. This ethnocentrism, which was identified earlier in terms of basing thinking on assumptions about an anthropocentric view of human/nature relationships, progress as linear, individualism, mechanism, and so forth, not only limits an awareness of other cultural approaches to sustaining the commons, but it also provides the conceptual and moral legitimacy for adopting a colonizing attitude toward cultures that are not based on these assumptions. In effect, the ethnocentrism, which is often the unrecognized subtext of new advances in theory and technological innovations, serves as the unexamined ideological basis for promoting the globalization of the West's industrial culture.

In my own experience of giving talks at universities across North America I continually encounter faculty who respond to my discussion of other cultural approaches to the commons by saying that we cannot go back, and who charge me with being a romantic. The claim that the current emphasis on multicultural education that is sweeping through colleges of education addresses the problem of ethnocentrism just does not wash, as professors of education have reduced it to learning about the eating habits, ceremonies, and dress—and little about the basic beliefs and values of other cultures. Their ethnocentrism is present in how they define the nature of individualism and freedom, in their assessment of whether the other cultures are economically developed, and in what they must do in order to become a consumer-dependent society. Like their colleagues in the more traditional academic disciplines, they also perpetuate the silence about the other cultural and natural commons.

The ethnocentrism that underlies most academic disciplines is dependent upon another myth that I identified earlier as part of the baggage of liberal thinking. This is the myth that language is a conduit. To summarize why this myth is so important to academics, and why it also helps to sustain the ethnocentric foundation of their theories and teaching: if it were understood how the linguistically based conceptual schemata of the culture (interpretative frameworks) influences thought it would be impossible to maintain the myth that knowledge (data, information) is objective—and that individuals (students and professors) are autonomous rational thinkers. The taken-for-granted root metaphors, which can also be understood as the mythopoetic narratives of a culture, influence thought, communication, and even the built environment of the culture. The examples discussed earlier of how highly esteemed scientists such as E. O. Wilson, Richard Dawkins, and the late Francis Crick rely upon the mechanistic root metaphor to explain their most recent scientific findings is simply one of many examples that could be cited.

Ethnocentrism, that is, the habit of universalizing one's own taken-for-granted cultural patterns of thinking, would be less of a problem if professors were to introduce their students to some basic realities about the languaging processes that sustain the cultural patterns that are re-enacted in daily life—and in the scholarly activities of professors and other types of experts. That is, students need to understand that words have a history, that they encode the analogies framed by the root metaphors that prevailed politically at an earlier time in the culture's history, that words (when organized into sentences) lead to theory about relationships and values that reproduce earlier analogies that prevailed over other analogies—and that individuals are largely unaware of how these earlier analogies influence what they may take to be their own original ideas and explanations. Students also need to be introduced to other cultures that are organized in accordance with different root metaphors or mythopoetic narratives. This would enable them to understand that their own taken-for-granted patterns of thinking and values are not universally shared. And perhaps this would lead to a more cautious attitude toward imposing our cultural values and assumptions on other cultures. Without this basic understanding of how the languaging processes of a culture reproduce earlier ways of thinking (and may serve to pass on to the current generation an earlier socially and environmentally destructive way of thinking) it is less likely that students will be receptive to learning about the nature and importance of other approaches to sustaining the commons. A recent example of how the taken-for-granted patterns of thinking underlie ethnocentrism that easily translates into imperialistic thinking is Peter McLaren's observation that to learn about the commons of indigenous cultures is like reviving the "noble savage" as the model we should emulate (McLaren 2005). And he is not alone in viewing non-Western cultures as less evolved than our own. It also needs to be pointed out that his ethnocentric pattern of thinking is an example of how the social Darwinism of the Victorian era continues to be reproduced by professors who, in so many other ways, are highly educated—except in a way that enables them to recognize how the language of their own culture continues to influence their thinking in ways that reproduce the misconceptions of the past.

It's easy to put these recommendations for reforming universities down on paper. But it is another matter to get faculty to change, particularly when they have been socialized to interpret their careers as building upon the cultural assumptions that few recognize as also being the basis of the industrial culture they often criticize. A small number have demonstrated the ability to unlearn what were the unquestioned assumptions. The majority, however, continue to view the ecological crisis and the process of economic and technological globalization as unrelated to their teaching and research. Even faculty that have made the study of changes in natural systems their central focus have not recognized that many of the cultural assumptions they still take for granted are major contributors to the ecological crisis they are trying to bring to the attention of the public. So the question remains: where do we begin if we are to move beyond writing about the reforms that need to be undertaken? How do we break through the culture of denial that is based on the misconceptions of previous generations of academics?

A possible starting place would be to engage faculty in a discussion of educational reforms that address the need to revitalize the world's diverse commons, as well as a discussion of how universities are complicit in the globalization of the West's industrial culture that is enclosing what remains of the commons. There will be a few faculty whose thinking will be based on Garrett Hardin's ethnocentric-based analysis of the "Tragedy of the Commons." For the most part, the majority of faculty will have been educated in the traditions of high-status knowledge mentioned earlier and will be unfamiliar with the nature of the commons. The smaller number of faculty that have tried to reconcile the liberal foundations of high-status knowledge with social justice concerns will be the most likely to be receptive to discussing how the revitalization of the commons represents on-the-ground ways of achieving social justice for the growing number of people now being marginalized and impoverished by the latest stages in the development of industrial culture.

As departmental affiliations often impede faculty from communicating with colleagues outside their department, and thus learning about shared interests, a discussion of the commons might be initiated by sending an e-mail that invites all faculty to meet at a certain time and place for the purpose of exploring the level of interest in carrying on a dialogue on the nature of the commons—and the educational reforms that should be undertaken in order to strengthen the commons as sites of resistance to economic globalization. It is important that the initial gathering not degenerate into disconnected comments, subjective opinions, and the sharing of misconceptions.

Thus, the following topics need to be identified as the focus of future discussions—along with the understanding that other topics might be added, and those offered at the outset might be dropped. The following list of topics is more likely to engage the attention of faculty by enabling them to recognize that the issues and questions raised in the initial gathering might lead to new insights and thus to the reconceptualization of certain aspects of their disciplines. This ability to recognize that their scholarly interests and courses would enable them to make a positive contribution is vital to whether the first gathering will evolve into an extended dialogue—one that might lead to fundamental reforms in what students learn in their classes.

The following represents one possible list of topics to be introduced at the initial meeting, as well as readings that will help keep the central issues in focus.

1. The Commons: In the Past and Today

    After general introductions and a brief discussion of the expectations of the participants, an overview of the cultural and environmental commons as they existed in the past and exist today needs to be presented. There should also be an explanation of the nature of enclosure, as well as introductory examples of the different forms it is now taking. The question of whether local, state, and the federal government can be stewards of a modern form of the commons should also raised. The latter question is especially important to ensuring that the discussion of the commons remains focused on today's realities and not on a romanticized interpretation of the commons of preindustrialized England. The purpose of the introductory discussion is to establish a shared understanding of the commons, as well as the nature of enclosure.

2. Ways in Which Today's Industrial Culture Contributes to the Enclosure of the Commons

    An introductory discussion of the nature of industrial culture as well as the connections between the enclosure of the commons, the ecological crisis, and the spread of poverty will help to establish the importance of the commons. One of the purposes of this discussion is to obtain a clearer understanding of the current extent of enclosure in the dominant culture, and the way various forms of enclosure undermine the intergenerational knowledge that represents alternatives to a consumer-dependent lifestyle.

3. Threats to the Commons of Indigenous Cultures: Western Science, Technology, and Educational Approaches to Development

The focus of this discussion should shift to a consideration of how the World Trade Organization undermines local economies and democratic decision-making. It should also take up the issue of ethnocentrism and hubris that prevents many promoters of economic development from recognizing how their scientific and technological approaches to development undermine the cultural commons of indigenous cultures. The connections between conserving the diversity of the world's linguistic/cultural communities and conserving biological diversity should also be discussed.

4. Social Theorists and Philosophers Who Support or Undermine the Commons

This discussion should be centered on how the nature of the commons—diverse in terms of culture and bioregion, dependent upon the renewal of intergenerational knowledge that enables individuals and communities to be less dependent upon consumerism, patterns of moral reciprocity rooted in the cultures' mythopoetic narratives, and so on—raises the question of whether the Western ideologies of market liberalism (now mislabeled as "conservatism"), libertarianism, Marxism, and social justice liberalism support or undermine the commons. There should also be a discussion of whether Western philosophers have contributed to an understanding of the importance of the commons—and if they have contributed to a distorted understanding of it.

5. Role of Language in Reproducing the Ideology Underlying the West's Industrial Culture

This discussion should address such topics as the myth of language as a conduit in a sender/receiver model of communication; how the metaphorical nature of the languaging process encodes and thus reproduces at a taken-for-granted level of awareness earlier culturally specific ways of thinking that were not based on an awareness of ecological limits, and how the prevailing root and iconic metaphors continue to reinforce the mindset of the industrial culture that is now being globalized. This discussion should also focus on the root metaphors that foreground the characteristics of the commons. How public spaces are enclosed in ways that are part of the languaging process of industrial culture should also be considered.

6. Technologies and the Myth of Progress: How Computers and Automation Contribute to the Loss of Intergenerational Knowledge

   The myth of technology as a neutral tool and, at the same time, the
   expression of Western progress needs to be discussed in terms of
   how it undermines the commons. The major focus of the discussion,
   however, should be on the implications of how computers transform
   intergenerational knowledge into an abstract text, and on how automation marginalizes various forms of craft knowledge—and thus the
   role of work in sustaining the commons.
7. How the High-Status Knowledge Promoted by Western Universities
   Undermines the Commons

   The nature of high-status knowledge, how it reinforces the mindset
   that is needed by a consumer, technology-dependent culture, as well
   as the forms of knowledge that are relegated to low status (and thus
   marginalized or entirely silenced) are central to the question of
   whether universities reproduce, in the name of progress, the cultural
   patterns and processes that are further enclosing the commons.
8. Social Groups, Policies, and Activities That Contribute to Sustaining
   the Commons

   This discussion should focus on the range of activities, social groups,
   and local and national policies that contribute to the nonmonetized
   aspects of community life—including the conserving of natural systems. In effect, this discussion should have an ethnographic focus
   that highlights the aspects of the commons that are alive and well in
   the faculty members' own community—and in other communities.
9. Educational Reforms

   This discussion has many possibilities that range from the double
   binds in the university curricula to constructive alternatives. The
   focus may be on how professors reproduce with only minor varia-
   tions the culturally specific, pre-ecological ways of thinking of their
   own professors—as well as on the absence of theory that explains the
   nonculturally neutral nature of technology, the failure to clarify when
   science becomes scientism, and the silences relating to the nature and
   importance of the commons. Other possible topics could include the
   need to rectify our political vocabulary in ways that enable students
   to recognize what commons-sustaining traditions are now being
   threatened by market liberalism and the reactionary nature of religious fundamentalism. The need to offer courses that present differ-

ent cultural approaches to sustaining the cultural and environmental commons, including how they are resisting the pressures to be integrated into the West's economic system, is still another possibility.

Making the commons the focal point of a discussion among faculty concerned with how global trends are impacting natural systems and contributing to the spread of poverty, as well as how the commons can be strengthened, should not be limited to what has been sketched out above. Additional topics and issues can be added or substituted, and faculty from disciplines as diverse as political science, sociology, history, philosophy, anthropology, cultural linguistics, business, education, and the sciences need to be part of the dialogue. And as issues related to the revitalization of the commons, as well as the forces contributing to its enclosure, are discussed an expanded vocabulary will emerge that, hopefully, will find its way into courses that have traditionally been devoid of any mention of the commons. Indeed, it might even lead to some traditional course content being reorganized so that the commons becomes the central theme, with the more traditional issues and explanatory frameworks being analyzed in terms of their impact on the commons. Hopefully, faculty in different disciplines will begin to realize that the revitalization of the world's commons can be the focus of an entire degree program—involving the sciences, social sciences, humanities, and professional studies. The rate of environmental change that scientists are now bringing to our attention, as well as the increasing number of people who are sinking further into poverty, make these changes increasingly necessary.

References

Abrams, David. 1996. *The Spell of the Sensuous: Perception and Language in a More-Than-Human World*. New York: Pantheon Books.

Alexander, Richard. 1987. *The Biology of Moral Systems*. Hawthorne, NY: A. de Gruyten.

Batalla, Guillermo Bonfil. 1996. *Mexico Profundo: Reclaiming a Civilization*. Austin: University of Texas Press.

Bateson, Gregory. 1972. *Steps to an Ecology of Mind*. New York: Ballantine Books.

Berger, Peter, Brigitte Berger, and Hansfried Kellner. 1973. *The Homeless Mind: Modernization and Consciousness*. New York: Vintage Books.

Bookchin, Murray. 1990. *Remaking Society: Pathways to a Green Future*. Boston: South End Press.

———. 1982. *The Ecology of Freedom*. Palo Alto, CA: Cheshire Books.

Bowers, C. A. 1987. *Elements of a Post Liberal Theory of Education*. New York: Teachers College Press.

———. 1995. *Educating for an Ecologically Sustainable Culture: Re-Thinking Moral Education, Creativity, Intelligence, and Other Modern Orthodoxies*. Albany: State University of New York Press.

———. 1997. *The Culture of Denial: Why the Environmental Movement Needs a Strategy for Reforming Universities and Public Schools*. Albany: State University of New York Press.

———. 2000. *Let Them Eat Data: How Computers Affect Education, Cultural Diversity, and the Prospects of Ecological Sustainability*. Athens: University of Georgia Press.

———. 2001. *Educating for Eco-Justice and Community*. Athens: University of Georgia Press.

———. 2003. *Mindful Conservatism: Re-Thinking the Ideological and Educational Basis of an Ecologically Sustainable Future*. Lanham, MD: Rowman & Littlefield.

_____. 2005. *The False Promises of Constructivist Theories of Learning: A Global and Ecological Critique*. New York: Peter Lang.

Brown, Joseph Epes. 1985. *The Spiritual Legacy of the American Indian*. New York: Crossroad.

Burke, Edmond. 1962 edition. *Reflections on the Revolution in France*. Chicago: Gateway.

Crick, Francis. 1994. *The Astonishing Hypothesis: The Scientific Search for the Soul*. New York: Charles Scribner's Sons.

Dawkins, Richard. 1976. *The Selfish Gene*. New York: Oxford University Press.

Dominguez, Joe, and Vicki Robin. 1992. *Your Money or Your Life*. New York: Penguin Books.

Esteva, Gustavo, and Madhu Suri Prakash. 1998. *Grass-Roots Post-Modernism: Remaking the Soil of Cultures*. London. Zed Books.

Freire, Paulo. 1973. *Education for Critical Consciousness*. New York: Seabury Press.

————. 1974 edition. *Pedagogy of the Oppressed*. New York: Seabury Press.

Gadotti, Moacir. 2001. "Pedagogy of the Earth and Culture of Sustainability." Sao Paulo, Brazil: Instituto Paulo Freire. 1–12.

Gates, Henry Louis, Jr. 1996. "Parable of the Talents." In *The Future of the Race*, edited by Henry Louis Gates Jr. and Cornel West. New York: Alfred Knopf.

Giroux, Henry. 2002. "Teachers as Transformative Intellectuals." *EDucate*: 2:46–49.

Hawking, Stephen. 1998. *A Brief History of Time*. New York: Bantam Books.

Haymes, Stephen Nathan. 1995. *Race, Culture, and the City: A Pedagogy for Black Urban Struggle*. Albany: State University of New York Press.

hooks, bell. 1994. *Teaching to Transgress: Education as the Practice of Freedom*. New York: Routledge.

————. 2000. *Where We Stand: Class Matters*. New York: Routledge.

Kelly, Kevin. 1994. *Out of Control: The Rise of Neo-biological Civilization*. Reading, MA: Addison-Wesley.

Kurzweil, Ray. 1999. *The Age of Spiritual Machines: When Computers Exceed Human Intelligence*. New York: Viking Press.

Light, Andrew, and Holmes Rolston III (eds.). 2003. *Environmental Ethics: An Anthology*. Malden, MA.: Blackwell Publishing.

MacIntyre, Alasdair. 1988. *Whose Justice? Which Rationality?* Notre Dame, IN: University of Notre Dame Press.

Marable, Manning. 2002. *The Great Wells of Democracy*. New York: Basic Civitas Books.

Marable, Manning, and Leith Mullings (eds.). 2000. *Let Nobody Turn Us Around: Voices of Resistance, Reform, and Renewal*. Lanham, MD: Rowman & Littlefield.

McLaren, Peter. 2000. "Gangsta Pedagogy and Ghettocentricity: The Hip-Hop Nation as Counterpublic Sphere." In *Challenges of Urban Education: Sociological Perspectives for the Next Century*. Edited by Karen A McClafferty, Carlos Alberto Torres, and Theodore R. Mitchell. Albany: State University of New York Press. 227–270.

McLuhan, T. C. 1971. *Touch the Earth: A Self-portrait of Indian Existence*. New York: Simon & Schuster.

Moravec, Hans. 1988. *Mind Children:The Future of Robot and Human Intelligence*. Cambridge, MA: Harvard University Press.

Murray, Charles. 1997. *What It Means to Be a Libertarian*. New York: Broadway Books.

Myers, Ransom, and Boris Worm. May 2003. "Rapid Worldwide Depletion of Predatory Fish Communities." *Nature*. 280–283.

Rifkin, Jeremy. 1996. *The End of Work: The Decline of the Global Labor Force and the Dawn of the Post-Market Era*. New York: G.P. Putnam's Sons.

Rothbard, Murray. January 2004. *The Libertarian Creed*. (Originally published February 2, 1971 in the *New York Times*.) Reprinted on the web site of the Center for Libertarian Studies. 1–16.

Sagan, Carl. 1997. *The Demon-Haunted World: Science as a Candle in the Dark*. London: Headline Books.

Schumacher, E. F. 1973. *Small Is Beautiful: Economics as if People Mattered*. New York: Harper Torchbooks.

Shiva, Vandana. 1993. *Monocultures of the Mind: Perspectives on Biodiversity and Biotechnology*. Penang, Malaysia: Third World Network.

———. 1996. *Protecting Our Biological and Intellectual Heritage in the Age of Biopiracy*. New Delhi: The Research Foundation for Science, Technology, and Natural Resource Policy.

Stegner, Wallace. 1992. *Where the Bluebird Sings to the Lemonade Springs: Living and Writing in the West*. New York: Random House.

Weaver, Richard M. 1998. "Conservatism and Libertarianism." In *Freedom and Virtue: The Conservative/Libertarian Debate*. Edited by George C. Carey. Wilmington, DE: Intercollegiate Studies Institute. 8–78.

West, Cornel. 1993a. *Keeping Faith: Philosophy and Race in America*. New York: Routledge.

———. 1993b. *Prophetic Thought in Postmodern Times*. Monroe, ME: Common Courage Press.

———. 1999. *The Cornel West Reader*. New York: Basic Books.

Wilson, E. O. 1998a. *Consilience: The Unity of Knowledge*. New York: Alfred A. Knopf.

———. April, 1998b. "The Biological Basis of Morality." *The Atlantic Monthly*. (Vol. 281, No. 4) 53–70.

Index

Abram, David, 18
abstraction, 116, 131, 146–48
AC3T. *See* Arts and Children Creating
    Community Together
accountability, 68, 75, 110
Adamah, 56–57, 62, 76
Adler, Mortimer, 34–35
African American community, 47–84,
    76; African American intellectuals
    and, 66, 75; organic intellectual
    traditions of, 70; self-identity of,
    62–66
African American Grassroots
    Leadership, 69
African American intellectuals, 62;
    African American community and,
    66, 75; natural systems and, 76
agriculture, industrialization of, 10,
    34, 39, 100
Alexander, Richard, 40, 42
American dream, 105
American Enterprise Institute, 157
Ames, Fisher, 130
Amish, 100–101, 104, 128
ancestors, honoring, 108
animals, experimentation on, 34
anonymity, 149

anthropocentrism, 31, 35, 79–80, 110,
    116, 125, 127, 155
Aristotle, 20
Arts and Children Creating
    Community Together (AC3T), 57
Asian American community, 60, 76
assimilation: consumption and, 65;
    critique of, 62–66; educational
    institutions and, 66; media and, 66;
    technology and, 66–70
asthma rates, 55
*The Astonishing Hypothesis: The
    Scientific Search for the Soul*
    (Crick), 121
automation, 10–12, 87–88, 97, 101,
    105, 166
autonomy, 32–33, 69, 82, 108, 118,
    124, 126–27, 133, 139, 151. *See
    also* individualism

Back Alley Bikes, 58
Bacon, Francis, 119
barter economy, 58, 103
basic needs, 87. *See also* basic services
basic services, 91. *See also* basic
    needs
Bateson, Gregory, 19, 42, 124, 136

Bellah, Robert, 131
Bell Curve: Intelligence and Class
    Structure in American Life
    (Murray), 135
Bell, Daniel, 118
Bennett, William, 34–35
Berger, Brigitte, 148
Berger, Peter, 148
Berry, Thomas, 132
Berry, Wendell, 132, 157
Biehl, Janet, 136
biodiversity, 14, 28, 35, 119
biophilia, 34
biopiracy, 14
Black Radical Congress (BRC),
    76–77
Boggs Center. *See* James and Grace
    Lee Boggs Center for the
    Nurturance of Community
    Leadership
Boggs, Grace Lee, 56
Boggs, James, 56
Bonifil Batalla, Guillermo, 4, 7,
    109–11, 132
Bookchin, Murray, 135–37
bootstrap economics, 58
brain, as machine, 28–29, 112, 124
Brazil, 91
BRC. *See* Black Radical Congress
A Brief History of Time (Hawking), 25
Brown, Joseph Epes Brown, 96
Brush Park, 52
Buber, Martin, 80
Buddhism, 110
built environment, 113
Burke, Edmund, 81, 102, 108, 130–31,
    157
Bush, President George W., 108, 128

Cajun American community, 47
Calhoun, John C., 130

capitalism, 70, 86, 135
Carson, Rachel, 123
casinos, 94, 97
Cass Corridor, 75
Catherine Ferguson High School, 59
Cato Institute, 157
change, 103; cultural context of, 38;
    empowerment and, 82;
    environment and, 41; industrial
    culture and, 39; progress and,
    21–22, 79, 108, 112, 155; tradition
    v., 37–39
Cheney, Vice President Richard, 157
Chief Joseph, 95
Chief Standing Bear, 94
Chinese American community, 75
Christian fundamentalists, 26–27, 30,
    37, 130
Christianity, 118
church, state and, 130, 135–36
civil liberties, 129
civil rights, 57, 70, 117, 120
climate change, 82, 87, 105
closed systems, open systems v., 111
cognitive development, 151
collective heritage, 131
collective voice, 60
colonization, ix, 34, 36, 43, 64, 79, 89,
    122, 126, 137, 144
Committee for the Political
    Resurrection of Detroit (CPR), 52,
    55, 75, 77
commons: affirmation of, 45; change
    and, 39; community-centered
    approaches to, 85–106; constituents
    of, 2; constructivism and, 150–54;
    contemporary ideologies and,
    107–38; cultural, 2; daily practices
    for, 137; decision-making and, 3;
    democracy and, 3; dependence on,
    2; ecology and, 43; education and,

85, 139–67, 154–58; enclosure of, 3–4, 17–45, 60–61, 93, 106, 122–23, 134, 137–38, 142, 150–54, 159, 164; introduction to, 1–16; natural, 2, 5; neglect of, 70–77; past and present of, 164; public policy for, 141; radicalism of, 1; renewal of, 139–67, 159; revitalization of, 60–62; sustaining of, 166; symbolic aspects of, 15; threats to, vii—viii, 2, 165; tradition and, 39; tragedy of, 3, 163; university reform and, 158–67; variety of, 36, 45–46; western cultures and, 89–93

communication, 61, 67–68, 143, 152

communicative competence, 44, 160

community activities, marginalization of, 54

community-based experience, 39

community-based models, 15–16

community-based organizations, 52, 72–73; corporate interests v., 93

community-centered approaches, 85–106

community-centered experience, 131

community-centered networks, 49

community gardens, 52–54, 101–2

computers, 68–70, 90, 122, 124–25, 129, 166; appropriate use of, 143; consciousness and, 148–49; constructivism and, 151; cultural neutrality of, 142–46; educational advantage of, 142; educational reform and, 140–50; enclosure by, 142; students and, 144–45, 150; usefulness of, 149

Concerned Citizens of Northwest Goldberg, 52, 58

Confucianism, 110

consciousness, 148–49

conservation, 79–80; by built environment, 113; by corporations, 108; of cultural diversity, 129; intergenerational, 108–9; by language, 111–14; by natural systems, 108–9; of traditions, 20–21, 109

conservatism, 81, 107, 115, 156–57; free-market, 116, 134; free-market v. mindful, 127–32; industrial culture and, 111; insights of, 131; liberalism v., 130; non-ideological nature of, 157–58; omissions of, 131; sub-vocabulary of, 116; temperamental, 114–15

Consilience: The Unity of Knowledge (Wilson), 23, 27, 121

Constitution, protection of, 157

constructivism, 36, 86, 150–54

consumerism, vii, 4, 53–54, 61–62, 70, 74, 83, 85, 90, 94, 99–100, 104, 128

contemporary ideologies, 107–8. *See also* core assumptions

context, 68, 83

cooperation, 53

core assumptions, 35, 37, 78–79, 117–18, 123, 130, 151, 155; critique of, 115; of industrial culture, 32; language and, 33; of liberalism, 136–37

corporations, 127, 131; community-based groups v., 93; conservation by, 108; universities and, 123

CPR. *See* Committee for the Political Resurrection of Detroit

Crick, Francis, 22, 26, 28, 31, 33, 109, 112, 121, 124, 162

critical reflection, 35, 78–79, 86, 122, 129, 135, 137, 150

Cuba, 102

cultural assumptions. *See* core
    assumptions
cultural diversity: biodiversity and, 35;
    conservation of, 129;
    marginalization of, 63
cultural evolution, 126
cultural identity, ecological footprint
    and, 66
cultural knowledge, 26, 48, 119–22
cultural maps, 19
culture: change and, 38; classification
    of, 140; digitization of, 147;
    ecological crisis and, 123; global,
    129; industrial, 2, 9–10, 15, 18, 21,
    32, 34, 37, 39, 45, 48, 53–54, 61,
    105, 111, 164; intelligence and, 32;
    language and, ix, 18, 19, 21, 33,
    162, 165; learned nature of, 125;
    membership in, 110; rejection of
    Western, 87; technology and, 21,
    66–67
*The Culture Denial: Why the
    Environmental Movement Needs a
    Strategy for Reforming Universities
    and Public Schools* (Bowers), ix

Daly, Herman, 129
Dawkins, Richard, 22, 26–29, 31,
    33–34, 112–13, 124, 161
debt, 127
decision-making: commons and, 3;
    local, 116, 133; participatory, 38,
    136, 151. *See also* democracy
decontextualization, 82, 86, 144
democracy, 44, 74, 160; enclosure of,
    93; local, 118; monetization of, 30.
    See also decision-making
*The Demon-Haunted World: Science
    as a Candle in the Dark* (Sagan),
    24–25, 121
Dennett, Daniel, 28

dependence, vii, 39, 138
Descartes, René, 20, 32
design, 113
Detroit Co-Housing, 58
Detroit, communities in, 47–84, 136;
    Adamah and, 56–57; auto industry
    and, 50; Brush Park, 52; Cass
    Corridor, 75; community gardens
    in, 101–2; discrimination and,
    50–52, 55; education and, 51;
    history of, 50; incomes in, 51–52;
    lead poisoning and, 51–52;
    Northwest Goldberg, 49, 52–55,
    60, 70–71, 75, 80, 83; Old Redford,
    49, 60; police and, 50, 54;
    Sustainable Detroit and, 57; toxic
    chemicals and, 51
Detroit Summer, 57, 59
development, 4, 126
Dewey, John, 18, 20, 32, 34–36, 79,
    86, 88, 114, 118, 129, 150–51
dialogue, 78, 83
Digital Library of the Commons
    (DLC), 141
Digital Millennium Copyright Act,
    150
discrimination: age-based, 88; race-
    based, 50–52, 55
Dissanayake, Ellen, 28
DLC. *See* Digital Library of the
    Commons
Dominguez, Joe, 104
drugs, 71, 90, 131
DuBois, W.E.B., 64

eco-justice, 3, 31, 44, 129
ecological crisis, 82, 115; capitalism
    and, 135; cultural roots of, 123;
    educational reform and, 35;
    educational roots of, 123; progress
    and, 137; references to, 83

ecological footprint, 66, 132, 160
ecology, 43, 125
The Ecology of Freedom (Bookchin), 135
economics, 155
economy, growth of, 128–29
eco-pedagogy, 151
Educating for Eco-Justice and Community (Bowers), ix
education, viii; assimilation and, 66; commons and, 85; Detroit communities and, 51; ecological crisis and, 123; enclosure and, 17–45, 138; industrial culture and, 15, 18; models for, 37; myth promoted by, 12–13; public, viii, 18, 133; race and, 63; reform of, ix, 15, 32–45, 45, 88, 106, 108, 119, 122, 124, 150, 158–67; university, vii, 18, 31, 66, 85, 88, 108, 120, 123, 142, 154, 158–67
educational reform, ix, 15, 32–45, 45, 88, 106, 108, 119, 122, 124, 150, 158–67; commons, renewal of, 139–67; computer-based, 140–50; ecological crisis and, 35; North American, 139
educational theorists, 62, 86. *See also* Dewey, John; Freire, Paulo; Piaget, Jean
Education for Critical Consciousness (Freire), 79
efficiency, 9–11, 149
Eliot, T.S., 157
elites, prejudices of, 17–18. *See also* core assumptions
Ellul, Jacques, 143
emancipation, 34–35, 49, 70–78, 82–83, 114, 118
Embry, Jim, 52, 56, 59
empiricism, 18, 120

employment: future of, 12; lack of, 41, 88, 90–91, 93, 99, 117; lifetime, 11; opportunities for, 51, 92
enclosure, 3, 33, 44, 122–23, 134; of biology, 106; computers and, 142; constructivism and, 150–54; of democracy, 93; development and, 4; education and, 17–45, 138; industrial culture and, 164; liberalism and, 159; progress and, 137; self-identity and, 60–61
The End of Work (Rifkin), 11
energy, sources of, 56–57
Enlightenment, 31, 33, 78, 120
environment: built, 113; change and, 41; knowledge about, 145–46; liberalism and, 122–23; libertarianism and, 135
Environmental Ethics, 19
environmental philosophers, 18–19. *See also* Berry, Wendell; Fukuoka, Masanobu; Light, Andrew; Rolston, Holmes III; Shiva, Vandana; Snyder, Gary
environmental racism, 76, 80
equal opportunity, 117, 120, 129–30
Esteva, Gustavo, 119, 132, 146
ethnicity, food and, 102
ethnocentrism, 23, 32, 36, 115, 121–22, 137, 160–61
evolution, 125; cultural, 126; metanarrative of, 153; monoculture and, 26–32; postbiological phase of, 29; time frame of, 41
evolutionary fundamentalism, 26–32, 34, 40
experimental inquiry, 35, 86, 118, 129, 150

face-to-face interactions, viii, 72, 74, 98, 103, 148

faculty, of universities, 160–64
The False Promise of Constructivist Theories of Learning: A Global and Ecological Critique (Bowers), ix, 140
FARM. *See* Foundation for Agricultural Renewal in Michigan
fatalism, memory v., 61
faux conservatives, 126, 128, 137
federal funding, 92
The Federalist Papers, 157
First Nation of People of Color Environmental Leadership Summit, 76
fisheries: depletion of, 87, 105; industrialization of, 10–11
food, 53, 61; diversity of, 141; ethnicity and, 102
Foundation for Agricultural Renewal in Michigan (FARM), 58
Foundation for Deep Ecology, x
France, 91
Franklin, Benjamin, 104–5
freedom, 78, 118, 133
freedom agenda, 76–77
Freedom Schools, 57
free-market conservatism, 107, 116, 134; mindful conservatism v., 127–32
free-market liberalism, 107, 116–19, 124, 126, 137
Freire, Paulo, 34–36, 71, 86, 88, 108, 115, 118, 123, 129, 150–51; core assumptions of, 79; limitations of, 77–84
Friedman, Milton, 81, 122
Fukuoka, Masanobu, 132, 157
future, prospects for, 32, 54
futurists, 22, 34, 37, 153. *See also* Kurzweil, Ray; Moravec, Hans; Stock, Gregory

Gadotti, Moacir, 35, 108–9, 123
Gardening Angels, 58
Gates, Henry Louis, 62–63, 68
General Electric, 11
General Motors, 11
general relativity, 25
genes: moral values and, 40–45; patenting of, 9, 14, 105–6; survival of, 34
Genesis, Book of, 110, 122, 125, 153
genetically modified organisms (GMOs), 5, 14, 100, 131
George, John J., 58–59
Giroux, Henry, 62, 77, 129
globalization, 21, 26, 35, 78–79, 86–87, 97, 115, 126, 161; global markets and, 129; workers and, 87–88
global warming. *See* climate change
GMOs. *See* genetically modified organisms
God-words, 78, 139, 151
going back, 7
governmental regulation, 128
grass roots, 15–16, 65, 73, 83, 117
The Great Wells of Democracy (Marable), 64
Greek traditions, 17–18
Green Maps, 141
Griffen, Susan, 132
growth, economic, 128–29
growthmania, 129

Hamilton, Alexander, 130
Hardin, Garrett, 163
hardwiring, 29, 34
Harris, Aurora, 59
Hawaiian American community, 60
Hawking, Stephen, 22–23, 25, 31
Haymes, Stephen Nathan, 62, 68, 71, 74–75
Heilbroner, Robert, 131

Herrada, Elena, 52, 55
high-status knowledge, viii—ix,
    21–22, 119, 125, 166
Hinduism, 110
Hobson, J. Allan, 28
*The Homeless Mind: Modernization
    and Consciousness* (Berger, Berger
    and Kellner), 148–49
homogenizing impulse, 64
homophobia, 81
hooks, bell, 62, 66, 68, 70–73, 75,
    77–79, 82–83
Hopi Nation, 61, 110
hubris, 121, 137
human purpose, 50
human rights, 159
Huntington, Samuel P., 114

IMF. *See* International Monetary Fund
imperialism, 139
indigenous American community. *See*
    Native American community
indigenous cultures, 47, 54, 93–98,
    128; going back to, 7; learning
    from, 8; liberalism and, 121–22;
    threats to, 165
indigenous knowledge, 14, 97
individualism, 19, 21, 31–33, 36, 62,
    69–70, 82, 108, 112–15, 118–20,
    133, 136, 139, 151, 154–55;
    liberalism and, 124–27; moral
    values and, 43; rationality and, 124.
    See also autonomy
industrial culture, 2, 21, 34; change
    and, 39; conservatism and, 111;
    core assumptions of, 32;
    dependence on, 37, 39; educational
    institutions and, 15, 18; enclosure
    and, 164; marginalization by,
    53–54; monoculture and, 48; myths
    of, 105; progress and, 9–10;

psychological impact of, 61;
    resistance to, 45; variety of, 45
industrialization, 5; of agriculture, 10,
    34, 39, 100; of animals, 34; of cul-
    ture, 2, 9–10, 15, 18, 21, 32, 34, 37,
    39, 45, 48, 53–54, 61, 105, 111, 164;
    of fishing, 10–11. *See also* enclosure;
    monetization; privatization
Industrial Revolution, 8, 78
Information Age, 152
information technology, 8–9. *See also*
    computers
insecurity, 6, 8–9
Instituto Paulo Freire, 35
intellectual property rights, 14, 150
intelligence, culture and, 32
interdependence, 44, 80, 82, 125
intergenerational connection, 94–97,
    127
intergenerational exchange, 53
intergenerational knowledge, viii,
    12–14, 20, 62, 83, 102–3, 129, 132,
    136, 139
intergenerational narratives, 72, 147
intergenerational responsibility, 108,
    126–27
intergenerational support, 41–42
International Monetary Fund (IMF), 6,
    13
Internet, 142, 150
interpretive frameworks, 19, 33
In the Spell of the Sensuous (Abram),
    18
Islam, 110
Islamic fundamentalists, 26–27, 30,
    130

Jackson, Wes, 132
James and Grace Lee Boggs Center
    for the Nurturance of Community
    Leadership, 52, 55–59, 70, 75

Kellner, Hansfield, 148
Kelly, Kevin, 30
Kepler, Johannes, 33, 112, 119, 124
knowledge: commodification of, 145;
  cultural, 26, 48, 119–22; diversity
  of, 17; about environment, 145–46;
  high-status, viii—ix, 21–22, 119,
  125, 166; indigenous, 97; intergenerational, viii, 12–14, 20, 62,
  83, 102–3, 129, 132, 136, 139;
  local, 39, 145–46; low-status, 119;
  objective, 22, 32, 126, 152; one-
  true source of, 23–26; place-based,
  20, 96; print-based, 67–68, 131,
  144; print v. spoken, 17; scientific,
  96–97
knowledge workers, 11
Kurzweil, Ray, 22, 27–29, 33

laissez-faire liberalism. *See* free-
  market liberalism
Lakota, 94–95
land ethic, 123
Land Institute, 100
language, 44, 61, 69, 118, 121, 152,
  161; conservation by, 111–14; core
  assumptions and, 33; cultural
  reproduction and, ix, 18, 19, 21, 33,
  162, 165; history of, 162;
  liberalism and, 124–27; tradition
  and, 159
Latino/Chicano American community,
  60, 76
Lead Busters, 52, 58
lead poisoning, 51–52
learning, from other cultures, 93
Lenin, Vladimir, 114
Leopold, Aldo, 123
Lerner, Rabbi Michael, 82
Lester, J.C., 136

*Let Nobody Turn Us Around: Voices of
  Resistance, Reform and Renewal*
  (Mulling), 76
LETS. *See* local exchange trading
  systems
*Let Them Eat Data: How Computers
  Affect Education, Cultural
  Diversity, and the Prospects of
  Ecological Sustainability* (Bowers),
  ix, 68, 144
liberalism, 70, 81, 107, 111, 115–16,
  119; conservatism v., 130; core
  assumptions of, 136–37; cultural
  knowing, misconceptions about,
  119–22; enclosure and, 159;
  environment, misconceptions
  about, 122–23; fathers of, 137;
  free-market, 107, 116–19, 124, 126,
  137; indigenous cultures and,
  121–22; individualism,
  misconceptions about, 124–27;
  insensitivity of, 121; language,
  misconceptions about, 124–27;
  origins of, 158; social justice, 107,
  116–19, 124, 126–27, 137;
  traditions, misconceptions of,
  119–22; universities and, 156
libertarianism, 107–8, 116, 120;
  environment and, 135; mindful
  conservatism v., 132–38
Light, Andrew, 18
light pollution, 5
Limbaugh, Rush, 108, 122, 128
local decision making, 116, 133
local democracy, 118
local exchange trading systems
  (LETS), 103–4
local knowledge, 39, 145–46
Locke, John, 18, 20, 32, 114, 118–20,
  122, 135

low-status knowledge, 119
Lyons, Oren, 96

machine: brain as, 28–29, 112, 124;
  universe as, 33
MacIntyre, Alasdair, 18, 131
Mander, Jerry, 132
Maori, 110
Mao Zedong, 114
Marable, Manning, 62–65, 68–70,
  72–73, 75, 82–83
Marx, Karl, 80, 114–15, 137
Maybeck, Bernard, 113
McLaren, Peter, 65, 77, 162
mechanism, 125, 155, 162
media, 66–68, 97, 99, 104, 117
memes, 29
memory, fatalism v., 61
Mennonites, 100–101, 128
mentoring, 19, 39, 54, 83, 147, 152–53
Merchant, Carolyn, 136
Midlands, England, 48
military intervention, 92–93
Miller, Charles, 59
Mill, John Stuart, 114, 118–19, 135
Mills, Stephanie, 132
mind-embodied-aesthetic-
  participatory experiences, 147
mindful conservatism, 107–8, 117,
  119, 122, 125, 130; free-market
  conservatism v., 127–32;
  libertarianism v., 132–38
*Mindful Conservatism: Rethinking the
  Ideological and Educational Basis
  for an Ecologically Sustainable
  Future* (Bowers), ix, 107, 118
monetization, 5, 30. *See also*
  enclosure; privatization
monetized activities, non-monetized
  activities v., 86–93

money economy, 91, 132. *See also*
  monetization
money, work and, 90–91, 105
monoculture, 129, 142; evolution and,
  26–32; industrial culture as, 48
Monocultures of the Mind (Shiva),
  23
Monsanto, 39
moral ecology, 43
moral reciprocity, 94, 97, 123, 128,
  153–54, 156
Moravec, Hans, 28–29, 153
Motor City Blight Busters, 58–59
Muir, John, 123
Mulling, Leigh, 76
municipalism, 135
Murray, Charles, 135
mutual exchange systems. *See* mutual
  support systems
mutual support systems, 49, 90
myth: of industrial culture, 105; of
  objective knowledge, 152; of
  progress, 6–7, 87, 137, 166
mythopoetic narratives, 41, 45, 69,
  110, 113, 122, 125, 153–54, 162

NAFTA. *See* North American Free
  Trade Agreement
Native American community, 60, 76,
  93–98
natural selection, 27–28, 34, 40–45,
  121
natural systems: African American
  intellectuals and, 76; conservation
  by, 108–9; management approach
  to, 146; romantic thinking and, 86;
  sacredness of, 97; self-renewal of,
  106; variety of, 47
need, sense of, 7
neem tree, 14

neoliberalism, 9, 13, 28, 37, 72, 86. *See also* liberalism
Newton, Isaac, 25, 33, 119, 124
Newton, Juanita, 52, 55
New York City, 101
Nez Perce, 95
noble savage, 162
noise pollution, 5
non-monetized activities, monetized activities v., 86–93
Norberg-Hodge, Helena, 132
North American Free Trade Agreement (NAFTA), 100, 120
Northwest Goldberg, 49, 52–55, 60, 70–71, 75, 80, 83
Nozick, Robert, 136

Oakshott, Michael, 157
Oaxaca, 136
Oba, Jorge Ishizawa, 132
objective knowledge, 22, 32, 126, 152
Old Redford, 49, 60
Onondaga Nation, 96
open systems, closed systems v., 111
oppression, 152
oral traditions, 154
Oregon, 47, 136
The Oregon Trail, 144
outsourcing, 9, 12–13, 86–87, 105
ownership, 134

Park, Kyong, 56
particle physics, 25
patenting, of genes, 9, 14, 105–6
patriarchy, 110, 147
Pedagogy of the Oppressed (Freire), 77
personal memory, 68
personal pronoun, 61
perspectivism, 120

pharmaceutical industry, 7
Piaget, Jean, 36, 88, 118, 150–51
place: development of, 47–48; experience of, 94; knowledge of, 20, 96
place-based knowledge, 20, 96
planetary citizenship, 151
planetary consciousness, 109, 126
Plato, 17, 20, 32, 155
police, 50, 54
political thought, history of, 130
pollution, 5
postindustrial society, 58, 62, 71, 75, 80, 90–93
poverty, 15, 32, 51, 54, 80, 132
power, centralization of, 48
Power of Ideas Book Club, 58
Prakash, Madhu Suri, 119
prejudices, 48
Principles of Unity, 76
print-based knowledge, 17, 67–68, 131, 144
printing press, 120
privatization, 5, 13–14, 55. *See also* enclosure; monetization
progress, 33, 115, 123, 126–27; change and, 21–22, 79, 108, 112, 155; ecological crisis and, 137; enclosure and, 137; industrial culture and, 9–10; linear nature of, 31, 34–35, 79, 118, 125, 155; myth of, ix, 6–7, 87, 137, 166; technology and, 120, 166; tradition v., 111, 120
property rights, 14, 134–35
Prophetic Thoughts in Postmodern Times (West), 81
psychological impact, of industrial culture, 61
psychology, 155
Public Art Workz, 59

public education, 18, 85, 88, 108, 120, 133
public services, 51, 54, 80
public spaces, 74
Puryear, Michael, 98

Quechua, 3, 48, 95, 110, 146
Qutb, Sayyid, 26

racism, 70, 75–76, 81
Randolph, John, 130
rationality, 17–18, 20, 32, 121, 124, 126, 133–36
reciprocity, 54
Red Jacket, 96
redlining, 50
reductionism, 25, 44
reform, 32–45
relationships, 43–44
relativism, 44
Religions of the World and Ecology, 153
Remaking Society: Pathways to a Green Future (Bookchin), 135
revitalization: other approaches to, 93–106; significance of, 60–62
Rifkin, Jeremy, 11, 91–92
Rivera, Julio Vallodolid, 132
Robin, Vickie, 104
Rolston, Holmes III, 18
romantic thinking, viii, 85–86, 86
Roosevelt, Theodore, 123
rootedness, 47–48, 96
root metaphors, 33–34, 125, 161–62
Rorty, Richard, 17, 32
Rossiter, Clinton, 81, 131, 157
Roszak, Theodore, 144
Rothbard, Murray, 133–34, 136
Rousseau, Jean-Jacque, 119
Rove, Karl, 128
rural communities, 74

Russ, Joel, 103

Sagan, Carl, 22–26, 121
Schumacher, E.F., 7, 15, 54
scientific knowledge, 96–97
scientific method, 22
scientism, 22–26, 31, 34, 81, 113, 118
segregation, 64
self-actualization, spaces of, 74
self-creation, 118
self-determination, 83
self-expression, 101
self-identity, 60–61, 72
self-reliance, 90, 120. *See also* self-sufficiency
self-sufficiency, 6, 53–54, 56, 59, 82, 101–3, 132
sender-receiver model, of communication, 67–68, 143, 152
seventh generation, 96, 108
sexism, 81
Shakers, 98
Shils, Edward, 122
Shiva, Vandana, 14, 23, 132, 157
Sierra Club, of Detroit, 58
Sim Earth, 144–45
Simmons, Charles, 52, 55, 77
Slow Food, 141
small businesses, 74–75, 98–99
Small is Beautiful (Schumacher), 7
small-scale producers, 98–100
Smith, Adam, 50, 114, 119, 122, 135
Smith, Brenda, 52, 55
Snyder, Gary, 95, 157
Social Darwinism, 28, 118, 121, 153, 162
social justice, 49, 82, 130, 151; ecological footprint and, 66; liberalism and, 107, 116–19, 124, 126–27, 137

social justice liberalism, 107, 116–19, 124, 126–27, 137
social security, 117
software programs, 144–45
specialization, 134
Spencer, Herbert, 118
spirituality, 94–97
spoken knowledge, 17
Spretnak, Charlene, 132
state, church and, 130, 135–36
Statute of Merton, 3
Stegner, Wallace, 47, 49
stewardship, 94
Stock, Gregory, 153
stories, telling, 53
students, 156, 162; computers and, 144–45, 150; experience of, 152; socialization of, 21; uninformed nature of, 19
subsistence economy, 4
Suez Lyonaise des Eaux, 14
survival: of fittest, 4, 28, 153; machines, 29, 112; unit of, 42
Sustainable Detroit, 57
Suzuki, David, 132
Swimme, Brian, 28

The Talented Tenth (DuBois), 64
Teaching to Transgress: Education as the Practice of Freedom (hooks), 77
The Technological Society (Ellul), 143
technology, ix, 6, 86, 90, 111, 128, 165; assimilation and, 66–70; consciousness and, 148–49; culture and, 21, 66–67; dependence and, 39, 138; ecologically informed, 58; individual subjectivity and, 66–67; progress and, 120, 166; workers and, 78

techno-utopianism, 1, 27, 35, 88
temperamental conservatism, 114–15
theory of everything, 25, 29
Thoreau, Henry David, 123
tools, access to, 99
totalizing regimes, 20
toxic chemicals, 51, 105
traditionalism, 81, 158
traditions: awareness of, 44; change v., 37–39; conservation of, 20–21, 109; critical rationality v., 122; emancipation from, 118; language and, 159; liberalism and, 119–22; modification of, 38; as oppression, 152; oral, 154; overturning of, 151; perception of, 121; progress v., 111, 120
tragedy, of commons, 3, 163
transformative learning, 86, 115, 129, 150
transportation, 50, 54, 91
Trojan Horse, 36, 49, 88

unemployment, 41, 88, 90–91, 93, 99, 117
United States, government of, 30
universality, of solutions, 49
universities, 18, 31, 85, 88, 108, 120; challenge to, vii; corporations and, 123; faculty of, 160–64; greening of, 154; online degrees and, 142; reform of, 158–67
urban agriculture, 101–2
urban space, 74

values: genes and, 40–45; individualism and, 43; market oriented activities and, 86–87; natural selection and, 40–45
Vasquez, Grimaldo Rengifo, 132

Victor Company, 11
visual messages, 67–68
Vivendi Environment, 14
voluntary simplicity, 104–5

water, 5, 13–14, 41, 57, 87, 91
wealth, 71, 113, 126
Weaver, Richard, 132–33
Weitzman, Martin, 28
West, Cornel, 62, 66, 68, 70–75, 78–79, 81–83, 102
Western culture, rejection of, 87
Western science, 96–97, 165
Whose Justice? Which Rationality? (MacIntyre), 18
Wilson, E.O., 22–23, 26–27, 29, 31, 33–34, 42, 109, 112–13, 121, 124, 161
Wilson, Irene, 28
wisdom, 7, 87, 96
Wolf, Arthur, 28

work, 67, 75, 98–101; craft and, 101; hand labor and, 101; money and, 90–91, 105; specialization and, 134
workers, 98–101; automation and, 87–88; displacement of, 11; exploitation of, 120; gains for, 90; globalization and, 87–88; real earnings of, 11; rights of, 117, 129; technology and, 78
World Bank, 6
World Trade Organization (WTO), vii, 6, 9, 13, 120, 153
WTO. *See* World Trade Organization

Young, Coleman, 51
Your Money or Your Life (Dominguez and Robin), 104–5

Zapatistas, 69
Zapotec, 146

About the Author

C. A. Bowers holds a Ph. D. from the University of California, has taught at the University of Oregon and Portland State University, and was granted emeritus status in 1998. He has published more than 95 articles, 12 chapters in other books, and 16 of his own books. He is currently Adjunct Professor of Environmental Studies at the University of Oregon.